SCOTLAND

BEYOND THE BAGPIPES

"This beautifully written book makes me want to jump on the train right now and head north of the border to follow in Helen Ochyra's footsteps. Truly compelling."

Jane Knight, former travel editor of the *Times*

"This lively and illuminating read is a must for anyone who loves Scotland or wants to get to know it better."

Natasha Foges, editor of *Britain* magazine

"Capturing a moment in time in pre-Brexit British history, Helen Ochyra writes about Scotland with the same warmth she finds among those she meets on her travels.

Not just a travelogue that gets under the skin of some of the country's untrammelled spots, including Rannoch Moor and Fife's East Neuk, Scotland Beyond the Bagpipes examines the cultural heart of a nation and our response to it.

But, above all, this is a miss-your-bus-stop travel narrative that whisks you along with lobster suppers, scenic drives and cosy B&Bs."

Laura Jackson, editor of *LoveExploring.com*

"Ochyra writes with wit and charm, bringing to the page many of the nuances of Scottish life that are every bit as appealing as the country's more obvious attractions."

Sally Coffey, editor of *Scotland* magazine

If you've ever wondered what makes Scotland so special, this book gets to the heart of it. It's more than a love letter to the country – it blends history, nostalgia, culture and quotes in one glorious read that makes you want to hop on the first train to the islands, cities, mountains and people that the writer so clearly adores.

Meera Dattani, editor of *Adventure.com*

SCOTLAND

BEYOND THE BAGPIPES

Helen Ochyra

The Book Guild Ltd

First published in Great Britain in 2020 by
The Book Guild Ltd
9 Priory Business Park
Wistow Road, Kibworth
Leicestershire, LE8 0RX
Freephone: 0800 999 2982
www.bookguild.co.uk
Email: info@bookguild.co.uk
Twitter: @bookguild

Typeset in Adobe Garamond Pro

Printed and bound in the UK by TJ International, Padstow, Cornwall

ISBN 9781913208103

British Library Cataloguing in Publication Data.
A catalogue record for this book is available from the British Library.

For Mum.
Because without you, none of this would have been possible.

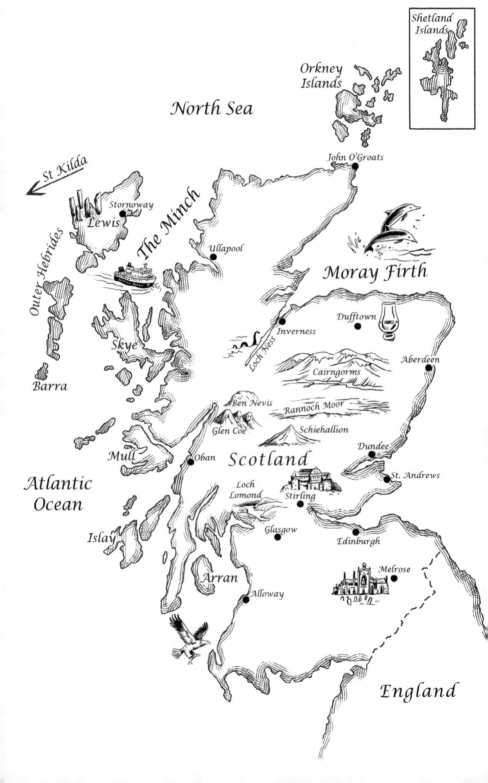

Contents

Prologue

It was back in 2005 that I first discovered Scotland. At least, I thought I did.

Like so many people who live south of the border in England, I had decided that I knew Scotland. It was part of Britain after all, a place that was more the same than it was different. I had pictures in my mind of bagpipes and tartan and shortbread, a vague notion that it was more mountainous, and wilder, than England. I imagined it to be fairly small, compact, easily tick-offable. It was somewhere that could always wait until next year. It would, after all, always be there. On my doorstep.

And so, as many other Scotland first-timers do, I flocked to Edinburgh for the Festival Fringe one year and expected to return home having somehow 'ticked off' Scotland. Neat and done and dusted. I was twenty-two and I only stayed for the weekend. I spent more time watching other English people performing monologues and stand-up comedy routines than I did talking to Scottish folk and I did not get any more than a mile or so from Waverley Station. Let's be honest: I didn't see Scotland at all.

And yet, even on that visit there was something unsettlingly magical about Edinburgh. Something in the way the grand Georgian buildings of the New Town gleamed in the rays of the sun as their medieval counterparts in the Old Town glowered behind the raindrops. A spell seemed to be cast on my undulating walk across ancient volcanoes – the story of getting from one side of the city centre to the other – and I was bewitched by the fact that the city's train station was named after a historical novel. I remember the clock tower of the Balmoral Hotel, glowing in the gloaming just above the station and lighting the dusky sky above me as I strolled from show to show. This clock is always set just a few minutes fast – to make sure you do not miss your train – and I never quite got used to it, feeling a jolt every time I passed as I imagined myself to be running late. On my final morning, I remember standing atop the peak of Arthur's Seat – a volcano in the heart of the city – and staring down the barrel of the Forth at the astonishing red lattice of the world-famous railway bridge. I left wanting more.

After that first foray I returned to Scotland dozens of times. But I always visited areas in isolation – taking the sleeper train to visit Loch Ness, or flying up to Glasgow. I was always on assignment, seeking a story for a newspaper article before speeding back to London to write it up and move on to the next item on the to-do list. In the pubs of the cities and the Highlands I heard tell of eight hundred islands, of a coastline twice the length of France's, of castles that could have been built for Hollywood – or for Harry Potter. But, as a travel writer, I could have told you more about the restaurants of Sydney or the bars of Bangkok than I could the twenty-three beaches of Coll or the eight whisky distilleries of Islay. Why had I for so long ignored the country immediately to my north?

I was constantly on the road – and then my life hit a speed bump. In October 2016 the earth shifted beneath my life, a force more powerful than a volcanic eruption and a jolt far sharper than any that the Balmoral Clock could bring. As the leaves shrivelled and fell, so too did my mother, dying suddenly and entirely unexpectedly after a brief, cold illness. At sixty-two she had been healthy and full of spirit. Having already lost my father as a child

I found myself parentless in my mid thirties. I was left with a house to sell, and a sense that life is just too short not to go on an adventure.

So I decided to spend a few months in Scotland, finally getting to those places I had sped past the signposts for or flown over on previous trips. Arrogantly I thought that I could see it all. With the smugness of a traveller who feels they can 'do' a country in one trip, I fell into the classic trap of thinking I could somehow tick off everything in three months.

Then I started plotting my route. In a heady rush of excitement the unfolded map spread across my kitchen table seemed to expand with every crackle of the paper beneath my fingers. Names like Glen Coe and Castlebay leapt out and before my eyes formed landscapes of deep glens and towering castles, while fantastical-sounding places like Achiltibuie and Dunvegan lit my imagination and seemed to come with a rousing, filmic soundtrack.

All at once it was screamingly obvious that I couldn't possibly go everywhere, up every mountain, into every glen and onto every sandy beach. Scotland had expanded in my excited mind and somehow I would have to narrow it down, find some boundaries. After all, nobody can visit eight hundred islands in one trip; even a travel writer with a serious love of ferries and powered by a geeky enthusiasm.

And then there was the matter of the divorce. Just three years before my trip, in 2014, Scotland had held a referendum. This vote was to decide whether the country should dissolve a three-hundred-year-old partnership. Yes or no. In the end the no campaign won with 55% of the vote; Scotland was to remain a part of the union.

That union is the one between England and Scotland, created in 1707 as a partnership of two countries, two equal partners. There was no conquering of one territory by another; this was a marriage – and the referendum was widely discussed as being a potential divorce. Yet all discussions in the mainstream media I was exposed to in England seemed to focus on whether Scotland could make it on its own. Was the oil about to run out? Would the country be allowed to join the EU? And what currency would its people use?

I wondered how an English person writing a book about Scotland might be received. After all, what was never really discussed in all the political hoopla was why Scotland might want out. What had happened in the UK to make one country want to leave? When your spouse says they want a divorce isn't the first question, "Why?" I realised with a start that this was the question I had never asked any of my Scottish friends. I was like the spouse who hadn't chosen to listen.

There has been no marriage counselling for England and Scotland, but I for one was keen to stay close, divorce or no divorce. Because whatever our politics, England and Scotland will only ever be as far apart as next-door neighbours. We may not have that joint account any more but we are sure to find ourselves popping round to borrow the hedge trimmer or share dinner and a bottle of whisky. And I for one will always want that bottle of whisky.

So I resolved that if England wasn't going to start listening to her neighbour, then at least I would. I wanted to understand how Scotland had managed to cast such a spell over me; why she had grabbed a hold of my heart and now would not let go.

With a boot stuffed to bursting with maps, books and waterproofs inherited from my mum, I left home in London and drove north. I was heading for the border. And, I hoped, the answer to my burning question: just what is it about Scotland?

CHAPTER ONE

North to Edinburgh

On my very first trip to Scotland I took the train from London to Edinburgh. Four and a half hours. At first it is all nondescript back gardens, graffitied brick walls, and fields dotted with cows or hay bales. But as you journey north it becomes more and more exciting.

In the last two hours before Edinburgh you skirt Durham, its magnificent cathedral sliding past the window. Then you pass through the heart of Newcastle, gawping across at the splendid steel arch of the Tyne Bridge. These are two of England's most enticing city sights, but it had always been Berwick-upon-Tweed that truly grabbed me; an unsung town just shy of the border that nobody I knew had ever set foot in.

It is the twenty-eight-arch viaduct that sweeps across the River Tweed here that does it. From the train it swings into view on the right-hand side, a marching arc of monumental stonework that carries the railway thirty-seven metres above the water, and is more than 650 metres long. It is hard to believe that this is not in fact the border. Not least because it's called the Royal Border Bridge.

The border itself is a few miles up the road but I had always wanted to stop in Berwick and have a good nose about. Such a grand bridge had to mark a suitably important town, I figured. And anyway, by the end of a seven-hour car journey I'll stop for pretty much anything. I might have stopped for a particularly handsome hay bale by this point. So I unfolded myself from the car, did a sort of overzealous yawn to work the crimps from my muscles, and set out on foot around England's border town. I was already primed to love the place from all those previous train journeys, but it truly got under my skin when I headed away from the could-be-anywhere high street along a path that led up onto the city walls.

Few towns are encased by quite such a well-maintained ring of ancient stone as Berwick, and it is possible to walk an entire circuit around the town atop its walls. Strolling a few metres up above the town centre on rolling, turf-topped battlements, Berwick seemed to be all church spires and stone merchant's houses. I took a detour between two grassy mounds and found myself striding out of their shelter and, quite suddenly, at the abrupt end of a tarmac path. My hair was instantly blown back by the breeze barrelling in from the North Sea. Waves rolled towards the shoreline, a smattering of white-jacketed bowlers ranged across the bowling green below me, and a jet-skier whipped up circles of white water in the mouth of the Tweed.

The makings of Berwick's historic prosperity were obvious. A trading port with easy links to Northern Europe and Scandinavia across the North Sea, it had a safe harbour for fishing boats hauling in vast catches of salmon, plus the wide Tweed River to access the hinterland for grain, hides and wool. In 1286, at a time when Berwick was part of Scotland, it sent £2,190 of revenue to the Scottish exchequer. This was about a quarter of the total tax raised in the whole of England that same year.[1] That's a greater relative contribution than London makes today.

Perhaps then it wasn't just a slight by John Balliol, the Scottish king, that led the English monarch Edward I to send the largest army ever to be marched north to Berwick just ten years later. The massacre of 1296 is estimated to have killed at least eight thousand people[2] – though some accounts suggest it was more than twenty-five thousand. It is said that for two days afterwards the rivers flowed red with blood, and that this was an act of ethnic cleansing – Edward's desire was to make Berwick English.

Today, technically, it is. Despite changing hands at least thirteen times over the years, Berwick has been a part of England since 1482. And yet the local football team plays (not very well, admittedly) in the Scottish leagues. There are Church of Scotland congregations. A Bank of Scotland sits opposite the restaurant I have lunch in, next to a hotel flying both the St George's Cross, the English flag, and the Saltire, the Scottish. Scotland's bestselling ale Belhaven Best is on tap. I feel like I might already have crossed the border.

The official border crossing actually sits just a few miles upstream, and here I find another extraordinary bridge. This is the Union Chain Bridge, namesake of my first night's B&B, Chain Bridge House – which also calls itself 'the last house in England'. Marketing spin being what it can sometimes be, I am rather surprised to find that it is quite literally that. From the front door I have walked just a hundred paces or so to reach the border – and the oldest suspension bridge in Europe.

This, frankly, is incredible. Not just the bridge itself – a sturdy stone and wrought-iron construction – but that I had never heard of it. When the Union Chain Bridge was built in 1820 it was the longest iron suspension bridge in the world. It was a pioneering design, and yet today it sits largely forgotten on a country road. Nettles and purple flowers I mistake at first for thistles have colonised both banks of the river, and there is not a person in sight. I pose for a selfie with the *Welcome to Scotland* sign before wandering back, still entirely alone, into England. This is a bridge that should be far more celebrated.

Back at the B&B I join the other two guests, a couple from

Manchester, at the dinner table. Our host Livvy brings us stew and we talk about Scotland, a whole other country that sits in the darkness out there. "I was dead against independence when they had the referendum," Livvy says. "Now I say good luck to them." The dreaded B-word is to blame. "After Brexit the phone stopped ringing. Bookings are significantly down. People have stopped spending."

On hearing that her daughter is seventeen (Scottish students do not pay tuition fees; English students pay thousands), I raise the spectre of university fees.

"Don't get me started," she says.

And it is not just Livvy's daughter who might think she would get a better deal if she lived a few hundred metres to the north. A poll by local paper the *Berwick Advertiser* in 2008 showed that 78% of people in Berwick thought they would be better off as part of Scotland. What is it that makes Scotland so seductive? I am determined to find out.

The following day I am set to reach the border once again, this time in a far more well-known and frequented place, on the A1 main road. As I reach the crossing point I pull into a layby and find a convoy of cars, campers and lorries parked up next to another *Welcome to Scotland* sign. Here dozens of people are snapping pictures of each other grinning and leaping in starfish poses under the sign. Across the road not a soul is doing the same with its English counterpart, and I wonder if I am not the only one pulled north by Scotland's magic. Perhaps Scotland is simply more exciting, more romantic, than England.

Scotland is certainly, it has to be said, friendlier. It is not that England is unfriendly – not at all – simply that Scotland is the sort of place where pretty much everyone will talk to you, and at length. This is of course a cliché, and one that I had heard long before I ever travelled to Scotland, but it was instantly confirmed for me on reaching Eyemouth. I had taken a seat in a chippy and was just deliberating over whether half a lobster would be enough for lunch when the woman who was serving the tables appeared. She had a warm, cheeky smile, and no sooner had I looked up to say hello than she had grabbed me by the hand. "I love your nails," she gushed, before launching into a conversation about where I'd had them done and how I really should go to such-and-such a salon, where Kelly would have the best range of colours. This might sound like an odd, even invasive, interaction, but for me it was heart-warming evidence that travelling alone through Scotland for months on end was not a crazy plan. I would not be lonely here.

I would need to get used, though, to the quiet. I have always been a talker, the sort of person who strikes up conversations in a queue or even on the London Underground. And although in Scotland I would meet plenty of people ready and more than willing to have a good blether, there would be times when there simply wouldn't be very many people at all. This is a sparsely populated country.

I find evidence of this straight away, rocking up in Athelstaneford, which seems to be largely asleep. The village is home to the National Flag Centre – in my head, a substantial museum of a stature befitting Europe's oldest flag, the Saltire. The reality, it turns out, is a little different.

I have followed a series of brown signs from the A1 but in the village itself they disappear entirely. I am left crawling along the main street, watching the local primary school kick out for the day and peering left and right to see any sign of what I had assumed must be a much-visited museum. After all, the Saltire is proudly flown everywhere, from pole position at the Scottish Parliament Building in Edinburgh to the national football stadium at Hampden Park.

Perhaps in England, and certainly in America, this would be the large museum of my mental image. But this is Scotland, a country that rarely celebrates its achievements with the swagger other countries seem naturally inclined to. And so I was looking for entirely the wrong thing.

The National Flag Centre is in fact a tiny doocot (dovecote) out the back of the local church. If it weren't for the Saltire flying in the churchyard I never would have found it. The museum is here because during a nearby ninth-century battle King Angus prayed for a win against an army of Angles and Saxons and saw a diagonal white cross painted across the sky. Since this was the same shape as the one St Andrew had been martyred on – and this being the ninth century – he of course leapt to the assumption that St Andrew was looking after him and his army. He vowed to make Andrew the patron saint of Scotland if they won. You will guess, of course, that they did.

It's a nice tale of divine intervention but there isn't an awful lot more to be said about it. Which is perhaps why the museum is in fact a short audiovisual presentation inside the doocot. The doorway in is about as high as a hobbit, so that even I, at all of five foot four, have to stoop to enter, and inside a sign asks you to shut and bolt the door behind you. *Not bloody likely*, I think. Instead I leave it swinging open.

The light that half-heartedly reaches inside does nothing to detract from the galloping horses and sword-brandishing soldiers that are projected onto the brickwork around an ancient map of Scotland. The presentation lasts for three minutes or so and then I find myself back outside, wondering what on earth to do with this unexpected extra couple of hours.

The answer lies just across the fields, and it is a hulking great one. North Berwick Law is a volcanic plug that is often mistaken for the similarly shaped Bass Rock, just out to sea from here, and there is something pleasingly conical about it. It's the sort of hill a three-year-old would draw. It is also an easy climb – and one that has a signposted car park to boot. I head up the slightly worn path, enjoying panoramic views out over the Firth of Forth. I can see part of the Fife coast opposite and, peering down water, can even make out Arthur's Seat in Edinburgh, some twenty miles away. I am essentially looking at a relief map of where I am heading next, and as I look out from the summit I can almost smell the gannets over on Bass Rock. From up here it looks an entirely different shape from the conical law I'm standing on: straight-sided and flattish on the top. It is also a chalky white colour, the result of being covered in thousands of gannets – the world's largest colony – and their splatter. I resolve to wear head-to-toe waterproofs for my visit to the Bass tomorrow.

The next morning my alarm goes off at 5.30am. It also goes off at 5.35am. And 5.40am. Because I hate mornings and know how partial I am to a snooze button, I had set multiple piercing noises to go off. I hate getting out of bed full stop, but any time before about 8.30am leaves me grumpy, sluggish and muttering to myself after dropping things on the floor.

I just about manage to dress and get into the car, yawning and cursing the crack-of-dawn departure time all the while, when it finally registers in my sleepy brain that it is sunrise. I slope out of the driveway of my B&B, turn a corner and there it is, a great golden orb just straining to leave the horizon. Shards of pink and warm yellow light spread across the fields and I smile at how perfectly beautiful it all is. Maybe getting up early has its benefits.

The Scottish Seabird Centre certainly thinks so. Maggie, my guide for a half-day adventure out to Bass Rock, admits up front that the early start is her fault. "It's better light for the photographers. We used to run a shorter trip but we got day trippers who weren't enthusiasts and they didn't always treat the birds as they should. People used to prod the gannets to get them to rise up and flap."

There won't be any of those sort of shenanigans today. We number only eight and Maggie has us all under her watchful eye. I feel she needn't worry; a collection of Scottish and German gents have turned out with foot-long lenses and tripods, many of them on a repeat visit to the island. I am inadequately provisioned in comparison and tuck my entry-level zoom lens protectively into my bag.

Our journey over to the island takes about an hour. But that's because we stop to feed the gannets offshore, our skipper Jane throwing whole fish over the side of the boat for the birds to dive for. "Focus your lens on where the fish enters the water," she says.

Within seconds at least one gannet swoops from the pack above us, often several, and tucks its wings back to form a feathered arrow that penetrates the water like a bullet. There is no bellyflopping here; each bird risks its neck, literally, every time it dives. There are no second chances.

I set my camera to the sports mode I had forgotten it had and snap away. For the first time in several years my 'proper' camera – the one that isn't my iPhone – has been pressed into service. I try not to think about how long these images will take to upload to my computer, and how much I will agonise over which ones I should delete.

And we are not even on the island yet. That involves a rather ungainly leg lift over the rail along the boat's bow, a leap from boat to shore, and a bag of sand that Maggie sprinkles on the seaweed-coated steps to avoid slipping. From sea level we walk up a couple of hundred metres, through the ruined battlements and out onto a pathway lined both sides with gannets. As we pass they see only legs, and feeling threatened they open their beaks, ready to give a nasty nip to any leg not moving past quite fast enough. I keep close to the person in front and move quickly; some of the group take advantage of the plastic boards provided to keep nipping beaks – gently – at bay.

Once we are all gathered next to the island's old chapel Maggie tells us that we have three hours here. I look around at the hundred-odd square metres she has marked out with red-and-white chains and wonder how on earth I will pass the time. The woman next to me looks with alarm at her husband and mouths, *Three hours*, with raised eyebrows. For the rest of the time we are on the island she stands with her hood up and her arms folded, staring out to sea as if the gannets aren't there. I suspect she wishes it was her who wasn't.

After about half an hour I fear I am also losing the desire to stand atop a lumpen rock in the Firth of Forth surrounded by birds. The sun has gone in, the light has turned dull and the cacophony of the gannets is starting to grate. There are only so many pictures you can take of a gannet and for me, 'so many' turns out to be 452. I tuck my camera away and discover I have a phone signal. I start sending pictures to friends, then it occurs to me I could shoot a video – and the rest of the time on the Bass flies past as I mess about with slow-mo and camera angles.

My final day en route to Edinburgh involves a detour. I am heading into the Borders, which my car's compass tells me is more or less directly south, back towards England. This area is a somewhat forgotten part of Scotland. Along with its western neighbours such as Dumfries and Galloway, it is the part that many of us coming from the south skip over – often fly over – to reach Edinburgh or Glasgow, the Highlands or the Hebrides.

But we shouldn't. Because the Borders are also Scotland's frontier land, home to many of its greatest abbeys and grandest houses. Also here is the longest new railway line built in the UK for over a century. Always keen to hop on a train, especially a new one few have yet travelled on, I have decided that my journey around the Borders should be by rail.

Climbing aboard at Stow I find I am not alone in my desire to ditch the car in favour of the UK's newest railway. A couple visiting from England tell me they are staying in Edinburgh but using the train to visit Melrose and its abbey. So, it seems, is everyone else, and we are a jaunty group alighting the train at Tweedbank at the end of the line, and piling onto the bus to Melrose.

On arrival everyone seems to be heading straight for the abbey, which peers out over the town from above the protection of a thick stone wall. This must surely be one of Scotland's most beautiful ruined buildings. Dusky red sandstone arches soar on all sides, some of them lined up along what was once the nave of this vast abbey, others retaining the intricate spindles of stonework that would once have held stained glass.

It was King David who brought the Cistercian monks here in the twelfth century, but it was the later king, Robert the Bruce, who most made his mark on this place. Not only because in 1322 he gave £2,000 to rebuild it after an attack by the English king, Edward II, (an amount that was more than the sum of the entire Scottish treasury at the time),[3] but also because he requested that his heart be buried here.

So it was. Or at least it is assumed that it was, since Bruce's body, exhumed in 1818, was found to have sawn-through ribs, and a roughly heart-sized casket was discovered here in the 1920s. It is a grisly idea – that someone with only fourteenth-century tools removed the king's heart – but today this is a site of pilgrimage for many, and a moving sight. The circular stone now placed in the grassy graveyard shows a heart crossed through with the Saltire and the words: *A noble hart may have nane ease gif freedom failye*. This is written in Scots and translates into English as: A noble heart may have no ease without freedom. Standing several hundred miles from home, the wind picking up strands of my hair and the sun warming my face, I smile at the rush of how important that freedom is, and how travel allows us to grab it for ourselves.

The Borders are also another great Scot's chosen resting place, and a few miles' walk along the River Tweed I find Abbotsford, Sir Walter Scott's palatial home. It is hard to overstate the impact Scott's writing had on Scotland; his *Waverley* series of novels later giving its name to Edinburgh's railway station, and his fame kick-starting a worldwide fashion for all things Scottish. He even stage-managed George IV's 1822 visit to Edinburgh,[4] suggesting that the king wear full Highland regalia, kilt and all. Naturally, what the king did everybody else wanted to, and the kilt became a must-have in high society. "There's nothing so easy to invent as a tradition," Scott once said.

It is clear that Scott built Abbotsford as a temple to Scotland herself. Stepping through the front door I am immediately confronted with a vast fireplace carved in stone and inspired, I am told, by the abbot's seat in Melrose Abbey. Wood panelling covers the walls, and is in turn covered, down to the last few inches, in the coats of arms of Scottish families, ancient weaponry and armour. In a display case I find a pocketbook belonging to Flora MacDonald (heroine of Bonnie Prince Charlie's escape to France), and on the wall a gun belonging to outlaw and folk hero Rob Roy. Much of the stonework has been copied from ecclesiastical buildings around the country, and from the windows is a perfectly framed view of the Tweed.

In the dining room a cast of the great and the good (Disraeli, Turner, Wordsworth) joined Scott for dinners, but ultimately it feels like a lonely house. Scott's study still showcases his desk in pride of place, but rather than an inspirational room where great novels were penned I see a gilded cage, one in which Scott toiled seven days a week into old age to pay off the debts of his printing and publishing companies. His wife died in 1826, the same year his publishing company collapsed, and he was left alone to pay off a debt amounting to some £12.2 million in today's money.[5] He could perhaps have sold the house he spent so much creating, but it seems doubtful it would still stand as it does today if he had. With the house packed and several coaches parked up outside, Scott's influence on Scottish tourism continues. Fortunately, it wasn't just that debt that outlived him.

My final stop in the Borders is Rosslyn Chapel, somewhere that, had my trip been made just ten years earlier, would probably not even have made it into my thoughts. Very few people came here pre 2006 in fact, but then something remarkable happened: a film was released.

The Da Vinci Code is referred to by my guide as 'the Rosslyn miracle'. "It was partly filmed here," she tells me, "and after the film was released visitor numbers jumped from thirty-three thousand a year to 177,000." Such is the thirst for visiting places seen on screen that the chapel is packed and there is not a seat to be had for the guide's talk.

I wander off instead, because I have read about something even more surprising than the supposed 'Rosslyn miracle'. I scan the walls of the chapel and poke my head into corners but my search is fruitless. Fortunately, a sprightly guide named Neil sees me clearly seeking something and asks me what I am looking for. I resist the urge to say the Holy Grail. I tell him instead that I am looking for the corn. This chapel was built in 1456, several decades before Christopher Columbus sailed to the New World, and yet it is said that there are ears of corn – something not known here until after Columbus returned from America – carved into the ceiling.

"I'm dubious," says Neil, pointing up at the supposed corn carvings. "They could be corn on the cob, but they could also be bundled wheat."

I am disappointed to hear this but can't help but agree that the 'corn' around the arched window could be any number of things.

Neil has something else to show me, though. "The one that's most convincing for me is the trillium," he says, pointing out a triangular sort of plant with three leaves carved high up above the nave and attracting no attention from anyone else whatsoever. "It comes from America and it doesn't really look like anything else. The St Clair family, who still own the chapel, were very rich and powerful back then, so it's possible they could somehow have travelled to the New World and brought back plants with them."

If this is true it was perhaps a Scot who discovered America and not Columbus. It's a wonderful theory that can almost certainly never be proven – or disproven. I leave Neil to answer his next question. It is, inevitably, about *The Da Vinci Code*. A Hollywood blockbuster will always trump a real-life historical mystery after all.

CHAPTER TWO

Edinburgh

Is there anything more aerobically challenging than a ceilidh? This was the thought running through my mind as the sweat ran down my back and off my forehead, and another, then another, powerful hand took mine and spun me around a twirling kilt. I was in Edinburgh during festival season and so, naturally, there was a ceilidh going on.

A ceilidh is basically a party where you are expected – forced, really – to dance. There is no standing on the edges clutching a beer bottle here; at a ceilidh the fiddles and the pipes insist your feet into movement, and there is a caller, a sort of lord of the dance, who shouts out what step comes next with brusque efficiency above the din.

Brusque, but never rude. Even when the white-haired, red-kilted caller grabs my arm and pulls me under an archway made from the raised arms of others there is the flicker of a smile on his lips and a slight wink of his left eye as he yells, "Let's gang, lassie" and promenades me in a fast skipping movement down to the other end of the room. Before I can catch my breath I have been deposited there, my head still spinning as my hands are raised roofwards by the man opposite. I am part of the tunnel of dancing couples now, and am smiling like a loon.

Edinburgh – at least in my experience – is not the sort of city you can visit and not get immediately, intensely, tangled up with. I cannot visit without at least an hour or two in the Sandy Bells pub listening to haunting traditional folk music and expanding my whisky knowledge, and this time, with the incongruous interlude into my trip of a hen do, I will not be able to leave without one hell of a party. Or rather, a ceilidh.

Edinburgh got into my soul and my spirit on that very first visit to Scotland at the age of twenty-two. It rained the entire time I was here and, being a recent graduate with no real money, I had inappropriate shoes and spent most of the time with soggy, uncomfortable feet. But I loved it. Majestic, magnetic, enigmatic, Edinburgh has a pull no other city in Scotland can match. No other city in the UK, in fact. And I'm saying that as a Londoner who sighs with sheer joy every time I clap eyes on Tower Bridge.

The initial pull for many visitors is Edinburgh Castle, Scotland's most visited paid-for attraction. It is certainly enticing. Above the Old Town a dark and brooding volcano stands, its craggy sides reaching up to meet the smooth stone of the man-made walls that run around its top. It insists on being summited, and when I do I find that there isn't just one building in the enclosure here. This is a complex of historic halls and houses, many of them far more modern than those in the thicket of medieval streets below.

Nowhere in the city better epitomises why Edinburgh was the place that evolved to be Scotland's capital. Because the castle is no man-made stronghold; it is nature's work that made this the obvious place for monarchy and military to gather. That it can only be approached from one particular angle makes it easy to defend. The oldest building up here – the oldest building in Edinburgh, in fact – is St Margaret's Chapel, built in about 1130 by David I for his mother Queen Margaret. Once this was where

Scottish royals came to pray in serenity. Although today it's packed with tourists wearing audio guides – and was once pressed into service as a gunpowder store – it remains a beautiful space, with simple chevrons carved around the creamy stone arches and a barrel-vaulted ceiling in pale stone.

It does take some imagination to see beyond the crowds of tourists to the truly historic artefacts on display here. I am most keen to see the Honours of Scotland – the Scottish Crown Jewels – and so follow the throng into the exhibition that visitors must walk through first. I skip round camera-toting tourists snapping pictures of the models of historic figures and squeeze into a room that seems particularly dense with people. Smugly thinking I can bypass the crowd by taking my chance to surge through the door at the other end, I sweep through – and find myself back outside. I have missed the Honours.

I cannot bear the exhibition a second time and so deploy my nicest smile to excuse my way back in against the tide. Fortunately the guide has seen it all and merely raises an amused eyebrow. She doesn't uphold the no-going-back rule she's supposed to, and we stand side by side looking at the crown, sceptre and sword of state together. "These are the oldest set of Crown Jewels in Britain," she tells me. "The crown was last used in Charles II's coronation in 1649. Then after the union with England they were locked away. Thing is, people forgot about them. They weren't found again until 1818."

It is incredible to think that for the best part of two centuries Scotland's emblems of power were considered to be so unimportant that they were locked away and pretty much entirely forgotten about. It was good old Sir Walter Scott again who found the jewels, pushing for a search of the castle to find them and eventually springing open a chest nobody had thought to open for some time, to find the crown, sceptre and sword just sitting there gathering dust.

Almost 170 years later, the Honours still feel somewhat

hidden away. The room they are in is dark and dingy and I peer through the gloom, scanning the place for a stone. Although the Honours themselves are exactly the sort of red velvet and slinky gold confections you would expect any major world power to use when indulging in the pomp of naming a new leader, it is a simple stone that I have come here to see. And yet I can't.

I ask the guide where I can find the Stone of Destiny. She points into the case at an object just beyond the end of my nose. "That's the stone," she says. "We're very glad to have it back."

It doesn't look like much, this oblong rock about two feet by one, but it has been used in the coronation of Scottish monarchs for centuries and is sacred in Scottish history. It belongs right here with the Honours. And yet for centuries it was in England, brazenly stolen in the 1290s by Edward I and installed in a wooden chair to be used in the coronations of the English. The symbol of English kings being anointed on a stone believed to be sacred by the Scots is a potent one, a nasty slight that fuelled the fire of conflict between the two nations.

It was four Scottish students who finally ended the stone's unhappy sojourn south of the border, stealing it from Westminster Abbey on Christmas Day 1950. Yep, four students drove down from Scotland in the freezing midwinter and stole a precious historic artefact from one of London's most famous – and, you might have presumed, most secure – buildings. The heist involved crowbarring open a side door, one thief breaking two toes by dropping the stone on himself, and the gang breaking the stone in two as they struggled to free it from the chair. And if this sounds like the stuff of movies to you, you'll almost certainly get a kick out of the 2008 film *Stone of Destiny* starring Robert Carlyle.

The castle is at its very best during tattoo season. Every August a series of towering metal stands appears around the Esplanade just outside the main gates, forming a temporary venue for the military to prove once again that marching in formation really is the most dazzling spectacle.

The Royal Edinburgh Military Tattoo is a sheer joy to watch. The metal seats thrum with every beat of the drums. You can feel the rhythm in your bones. Your eyes dart every which way as you try to take in row upon row of pipers, each one wearing their sporran and carrying their pipes at precisely the same angle – and sporting exactly the same stoic facial expression. A typical line-up – if there is such a thing – might include fiddlers from Shetland, an army band from Nepal and a motorcycle stunt team with no member older than sixteen. There are always Highland dancers, of course, their kilts billowing in a dizzying whirl of colour as their legs kick and bend at the knee in the most improbably fast fashion, and every year the finale includes the lone piper, standing atop the castle walls playing the sort of haunting tune that makes everyone fall silent and listen. I defy anyone to rustle a sweet wrapper at this point. It would be as impudent as not linking arms during 'Auld Lang Syne'. Which, of course, is what comes next.

The whole thing ends with fireworks and a glow in the air, sending me on my way with the sort of warm-hearted bonhomie for all things Scottish I have previously associated mostly with whisky. This is the very best spectacle the city puts on, and that includes the multiple wonderful events that make up the Edinburgh Festivals.

The castle may be more visited, but for me it is the Forth Rail Bridge that really sums up Scotland's capital. It may be nine miles from the city centre but this bridge is Edinburgh's statement of intent. It marks the crossing point into the wilder north and it does so with gutsy aplomb. Just look at the accolades: the world's first major steel structure,[6] Scotland's largest listed building,[7] the longest cantilever bridge in Britain and the second in the world[8].

It took more than four thousand men three and a half years to build, and when it was opened by Edward VII in 1890 it was the longest bridge in the world. Its main span of 521 metres was three times longer than anything ever built before.[9] Before 2011 and a new type of paint, it famously took so long to paint the bridge that on finishing at one end the workers would have to immediately return to the other and start all over again.

But numbers don't have force when you see them on the page. And the Forth Rail Bridge has to be seen – properly seen from all angles – to really understand just how impressive it is. And so before leaving Edinburgh I have made time for a boat trip on the *Forth Belle*. We are heading for Inchkeith, an island in the middle of the Forth, but it is the bridges that everyone is excited about. Because of course it is not just the Forth Rail Bridge that vaults across the water here; it is also the Forth Road Bridge and the new Queensferry Crossing, which opened in 2017.

The significance of this place is hard to overstate and the commentary on the boat is almost breathless with trying to fit it all in, despite being pre-recorded. There are just so many famous and important people and events to get through.

What really sticks with me is what a lifeline this crossing point is. On my visit the Queensferry Crossing had just opened and the news was full of complaints about the traffic and how much time was being lost by people sitting in queues of cars. It turned out that a significant percentage of this traffic was made up of people coming along to have a gander at what has been called the largest Scottish infrastructure project in a generation. It is blooming impressive, and people had been leaning out of car windows snapping selfies, grinning in front of its three overlapping triangles of white steel cables, which reach down to the M90 like arms linked by held hands across the water.

But sod the new bridge; I remain head over heels for the oldest. The lattice of tomato-red steel that careers across the Forth is truly beautiful, and from my bobbing boat beneath it I find myself in awe. I snap away, trying to capture its vast majesty in one shot.

CHAPTER THREE

Fife

I love a brown sign, and so, it seems, does Fife. As soon as I cross the Forth and enter the Kingdom of Fife, I find my eyes pulled this way and that by chocolate-brown signs pointing out tourist attractions. They promise a distillery along this road, a beach down that, even a secret bunker at one point. I crane my neck as I pass each side road, wondering how much of a detour these places would be.

These signs are my first hint at how much there is to see in Fife – and that I might not have allowed quite enough time here. This is a part of Scotland few in England have heard of, and even the Scots haven't exactly embraced it as a holiday destination. There are a few coastal villages whose holiday cottages bring an influx of Edinburgh folk come summer (Elie in particular), but other than that it's mostly golfers who come here. I had imagined a couple of days would be enough.

On the first of these I had made time for exploring Dunfermline, a town precisely nobody told me I should visit. You could do far worse than Dunfermline for a weekend break, though, and it deserves far more than its paltry two thirds of a page in the guidebook I've brought with me. This is Scotland's ancient capital and it has a marvellous collection of grand old buildings, all within pleasant strolling distance of each other. Several kings were born here, the last of whom was Charles I, born in Dunfermline Palace in 1600. Today the palace is under the protection of Historic Environment Scotland, a public body that looks after Scotland's history by caring for its ancient buildings.

Many a Scottish castle would surely be rubble without HES. But without Robert the Bruce, Dunfermline Abbey would have been rubble long before it was the birthplace of kings. This is yet another building that was sacked by Edward I on his rampage north, and yet another that Robert financed the rebuilding of.

His heart may be in Melrose but the rest of him is here, along with fellow monarch David I. As I step inside the nave, sunlight bleeds in through the stained-glass windows, painting the vaulted ceilings of the side aisles a warm peach. It cannot quite reach the columns beyond, their chevron-carved thickness defiant in the darkness. It is a suitably grand place for a Scottish monarch to rest.

But it's not all ancient history here. Surely the most famous person to come out of Dunfermline is Andrew Carnegie, the great philanthropist. I had always thought of Carnegie as an American through and through, but he was actually born here in Dunfermline in 1835 and his birthplace is now one of the town's top attractions.

Carnegie only spent his first thirteen years in this wee stone house, in grinding poverty. Tiny beds, smaller than a modern child's bunk, are built into the wall of the kitchen, so the family could sleep in relative warmth. Crammed into a corner are a desk and a spinning wheel; a handloom dominates the only other downstairs room. Two families would have shared this space, both running weaving businesses from the house. The noise must have been ceaseless.

When the family's poverty was exacerbated by the Great

Depression of 1847, Carnegie's parents decided to move the family across the Atlantic. It was make or break, a great gamble that was taken by more than 2.3 million Scots between 1825 and 1938 as they also began to find their lives in Britain untenable.[10] It is said that in 1931 one in five Scots was no longer living in Scotland.[11]

The Carnegie family's gamble paid off. From his new home in America, Andrew built a coal and steel empire that would make him the richest man in the world. Not just at that time, but at any time since. So if you're thinking, *Well, I bet he's got nothing on Bill Gates*, consider this: at the time of writing Gates was worth around $86 billion;[12] today Carnegie's fortune would be worth a mind-boggling $300 billion.[13] That's more than Coca-Cola and McDonald's are worth combined.[14]

But Carnegie's story is not just a classic rags-to-riches tale. Carnegie is so fascinating because he believed that "The man who dies rich, dies disgraced." He gave away about 90% of his wealth, creating "ladders upon which the aspiring can rise – free libraries, parks and means of recreation".

Those libraries are his most famous legacy, and the very first was built here in his home town. A total of 2,811 were ultimately built worldwide,[15] but it all started here, and a few months before my visit, the original Carnegie library was given a sparkly new extension. Today, the café is a hubbub of local blether, a primary school group in matching red sweatshirts is slowly making their way through the local history section, and I have to compete for space in the galleries. Most of the elbow-wriggling is required in the gallery on home life – because don't we all just love peering into other people's homes?

Here I find three recreations of kitchens past. But we're not talking the eighteenth-century kitchen of Andrew Carnegie's birthplace, one that is unfamiliar to anyone alive today. No – here is a scene from the 1990s, electric carving knife, rotating spice rack and all. I scoff to myself that this could hardly be thought of as history, looking around for someone to back me up in thinking that this is a ludicrous era to have on display. But instead of finding another pair of incredulous eyes I am confronted with a trio of schoolchildren. "Wow, that kitchen is old," one announces. I walk off to look at the garden.

I was very keen to get to Fife's East Neuk. As far as I can tell, this is the only place in the world to be called a *neuk*, the Scots word for corner (or nook), and it has a reputation for storybook fishing villages and sandy beaches.

Those beaches begin more or less straight away, just five or so miles after you shrug off the M90. A sunny, blue-sky day and Aberdour's Silver Sands tempted me to wander awhile, looking back at the trio of Forth Bridges. This is one of Scotland's sunniest corners and I find I can pick out details on the opposite bank of the Forth (Bass Rock, North Berwick Law), illuminated by the low sun on one of those burnished-orange afternoons you only get late on in the year, and if you are far enough north.

Any drive around the East Neuk is likely to be slowed by the sedentary gait of a tractor or the sudden emergence of a combine harvester from a field. Hailing from Wiltshire, I am used to this pace of transit and I learn to love it all over again as I tour around; it gives me time to watch, on one occasion, a cloud of birds I could swear are forming themselves into the outline of one larger bird, swooping across the late-afternoon sky like a giant dove.

I eventually arrive in the wonderfully named Pittenweem. This is the East Neuk's main fishing harbour, and in the 1970s a day when one thousand boxes of white fish were landed was a poor one. Today no white fish comes in here, but there are plenty of langoustines, lobsters, crabs and scallops landed by the fishing boats I see quietly jouncing in a line by the quay.

The village feels like something out of a children's book. *Postman Pat by the Sea,* perhaps. The buildings are like toy houses, a stately line-up of natural stone and creamy white. A squat church peers out from above them, its clock face gazing out to sea. The boats in the harbour seem only to be painted brilliant blue or pillar-box red, and the quay is ancient stone, growing yellowy-green with lichen. On the harbourfront parking for fishermen is reserved and what would elsewhere be turned into more parking has been thoughtfully left as a turning place. I even find a block of public toilets, not only open but in the process of being cleaned. Everything here is trim and well ordered. It feels almost utopian.

Pittenweem harbourfront is as good a place as any to head out on a stroll along a well-trodden path that is one of Scotland's best. The Fife Coastal Path is 117 miles in total, but the joy of it is that you can easily tackle a short section without worrying too much about start and finish points. There are fishing harbours all the way along the coast here, and as you head along the northern edge of the Firth of Forth there is almost perpetually a village – another starting, or finishing, point to a walk – on the horizon.

I am headed for Crail, and if I step it out I can make it in time for lunch. I bound along the easy, well-formed path, watching seals watching me from offshore and looking over to Bass Rock. All the while I am dreaming of returning here to do the whole thing.

I arrive in Crail with only one thought in my mind – lobster. This is because Reilly Shellfish sits on the harbour's edge here, and although it is little more than a shed and a tank – with about a dozen fresh, still-crawling lobsters awaiting their fate – it is one of the best places in Scotland to feast on fresh shellfish.

Those lobsters' fate today is me, and I select my lunch with a pointing finger – held far back from the water, of course. My lobster is scooped out and held aloft by its haunches, if a lobster has such a thing, before it disappears into the kitchen to be cooked. I sit at the only table, a wooden bench overlooking the fishing boats, and lose myself in shellfish attack, digging into the claws with the smooth metal pick and pulling meat from the shell with my fingers. There is not a better lunch that I can imagine. And yet this is a fairly standard catch of the day in Scotland, where just-caught lobster is served from kiosks, shacks and stalls for the price of a burger in London. I foresee plenty more lobster lunches in my future.

I decide to walk back to Pittenweem the way I have come. I normally hate to double back on myself and walk the same path twice, but today I need to work up an appetite. Because my final night in the East Neuk is a few miles inland at the Peat Inn, one of Scotland's Michelin-starred restaurants.

The Peat Inn was the very first restaurant in Scotland to get a Michelin star, back in the 1980s when most people thought that Scottish food was – if they were being moderately polite about it – crap. Many people in England still seem to think this; just try talking to an English person about Scottish food without deep-fried Mars Bars coming up.

But I am beginning to wonder if this is just a clever ruse by the Scots to keep the best of their ingredients to themselves. Because Scottish food is wonderful. Yes, admittedly, not all of it. There are deep-fried pizzas and fizzy drinks that contain more sugar than a doughnut, but even the French have hamburgers and we don't accuse them of eating poorly. In Scotland there are plump oysters and juicy lobsters being pulled from the ocean, herds of beefy Highland cattle and deer roaming the hills, and even an extensive soft fruits industry that produces some of the world's best raspberries. There is fabulous cheese, and a fine tradition of smoking that extends far past the side of salmon you might treat yourself to at Christmas. In Scotland it is all about the produce, and eating well can mean devouring a lobster with sticky fingers on the quayside just as much as it can mean donning your spiffiest suit and tucking a napkin onto your lap.

The latter, though, is what the Peat Inn is all about. Dinner here starts with a G&T by the fire and an easy choice – that I simply had to have the tasting menu. It promised langoustines, after all, as well as something I had never had before: mountain hare. For me, this is the joy of a tasting menu. Would I order mountain hare as my main course? Probably not. But as part of a dinner that couldn't possibly leave me heading to bed hungry, why not? And it was wonderful. Gamey and served with truffle, it was the perfect autumn dish. "It's not a meat people are that comfortable with so we weren't sure how it would go down," chef Geoffrey Smeddle tells me, "but people seem to really like it." Scotland, it seems, always has something more up her sleeve.

I can't help but associate St Andrews with Prince William. The prince was born just a few weeks before me, and so his milestones have taken place at the same times as mine. Of course I know that the prince studied – and met his future wife – here. But that was a long time ago. Nobody, surely, is coming here now for the royal connections, and yet the place is absolutely packed, by far the most tourist-heavy place I have been since Edinburgh.

St Andrews is pretty far from everywhere and yet here you somehow feel as though you are at the centre of things. Not just where a prince went to university, but also where you can stand inside the largest medieval building in Scotland and play the world's oldest golf course.

I am no golfer but I find myself drawn to the Himalayas – better known as the St Andrews Ladies' Putting Club – a ridiculously undulating grassy patch of St Andrews' hallowed golfing turf. This is the sort of land that nobody in their right mind would build a golf course on, an area that reminds me of Teletubbyland or perhaps Hobbiton. Every time you hit a ball it curves off in exactly the direction you didn't expect it to, and as the eighteen holes are moved constantly there is no improving your game over multiple rounds.

I find myself transfixed by one hole in particular and, since I am getting ahead of the family behind me, I keep rewinding back to the start to try again – and again. I am cheekily breaking the rules but I am determined not to be beaten by what appears to be a magnetic field, pulling the ball round in a spiral to end up in the same place (the wrong place, obviously) every single time.

It is incredibly frustrating, though perhaps not as frustrating as trying to play the Old Course here can be. This is where golf was first played, over six hundred years ago. The course eventually settled on having, by accident rather than design, eighteen holes, making this the standard all other courses would follow. It has also hosted the Open Championship twenty-nine times. So it is, it would be understating it to say, popular. This means that you have to go into a ballot for a tee time, drawn at 2pm two days ahead of the day you want to play. How infuriating it must be to make travel plans for this once-in-a-lifetime round of golf, only to be told you can't play. This perhaps explains why there are six other courses at the Home of Golf.

Although plenty of people come here to play golf, plenty of others come to see the bones of what was once Scotland's most important city. Fife is called a kingdom because it's considered to be the very same land as one of the major Pictish kingdoms, Fib. The Picts – or painted people, so named by the Romans – were the direct descendants of the first hunter-gatherers to make their lives in Britain after the Ice Age,[16] and it was their king who established a monastery here at St Andrews, in the eighth century, as a home for the relics of the eponymous saint.

There's nothing to see of this now, but towering above the sea at one end of the town there is an almighty skeleton of a building; the building that was once the headquarters of the Scottish Church. St Andrews Cathedral is truly awesome, even in its now-ruinous state. Much of the enclosing walls remain and it is still possible to feel the size of the thing – wide enough, it is said, that Robert the Bruce was able to ride down the aisle of the nave on his horse.

The Bruce also held his first parliament here, while on his quest to become Scotland's legitimate king, and I can imagine why he chose it. Even today, with most of it gone, St Andrews Cathedral is an imposing place. I stand beneath an archway that must be three times my height, a chunky stone viewfinder that frames a gap-toothed wall at the other end of the nave. Windows long gone, it stands with blue sky behind it, two turrets pointing upwards in defiance of the years that have passed. There are dozens of people here but they have been swallowed up – there is just so much space in what was once Scotland's largest church. I am already feeling dwarfed by Scotland, and I haven't even got to the Highlands yet.

CHAPTER FOUR

Dundee and Perth

I love Dundee. For some reason, this tends to surprise people. Even people who are from there, who really should know better.

Because Dundee is strong and spirited and independent. It doesn't care that plenty of people down south think it's a dump (often despite having never been there), and it was the first place in the country to declare a Yes vote in the 2014 independence referendum. It also recorded the highest percentage for Yes, at 57%.[17] This is a confident city.

Dundee gives a great first impression too. On my visit, I park in a nondescript shopping centre car park and step out into the city to find a lovely pedestrianised precinct. In City Square the wooden picnic tables are packed with people sitting amid gushing fountains. A bronze Desperate Dan statue marches mid stride opposite (comic book the *Dandy*, as well as the *Beano*, hails from here), and the local *Evening Telegraph* is being sold by a man in a cap at a kiosk.

Inside the visitor centre a warm, smiley woman called Fiona hands me a map and covers it in squiggles and looping circles as she runs through everything the city has to offer. Dundee is

Scotland's fourth largest city but with a population of only a shade over 150,000 it's a compact place that Fiona assures me I can easily walk around, ticking off the main sights in a day or so.

At the time of my visit, V&A Dundee – Scotland's first design museum – was under construction and I wanted to have a nose at the new building, said to be inspired by Scotland's cliffs. So I headed down to the waterfront, where, right next to one of Scotland's most talked-about building sites (and, in my opinion far more boat-like than cliff-like), I found the RRS *Discovery*.

That this world-famous ship was here and that I had had no idea (before I met Fiona, of course) says it all. This was the ship that took Captain Scott and Ernest Shackleton to Antarctica in 1901, and it was built right here in Dundee's shipyards.

Throughout the nineteenth century and into the twentieth, Dundee was a major whaling centre. And so the city had plenty of experience in building ships that could cope with pack ice. Since *Discovery* would be headed straight for Antarctica, it wasn't a difficult choice to build her here in Dundee.

This was not the grim expedition that Scott would not return from (that was in 1912), but it certainly wasn't without incident. A young crew member fell to his death from the mast just outside Lyttelton Harbour in New Zealand, Shackleton contracted serious scurvy and spent much of his time coughing up blood, and the ship had to be blown free of more than twenty miles of ice with explosives.

But it was a triumph. More than five hundred new marine animals and fish were discovered, hundreds of miles of glacier, mountain and coast were mapped, and an emperor penguin rookery was seen for the first time. Crowds of flag-waving fans welcomed the ship back to Britain in 1903 and when the RGS eventually got through all that material they found they required ten weighty volumes to publish all of the trip's findings.

I climb aboard *Discovery* after reading about her successful voyage, and am astonished to find how small she is. As I walk across the main deck, an image of the forty-eight men, twenty-three howling dogs and forty-five terrified sheep reported to have left New Zealand on her runs noisily through my mind. *Discovery* was at sea for three years; I'm not sure I could have stood it for three hours.

Tales of life on board don't make for any prettier reading. There are stories of feet being crammed painfully into boots frozen crooked, powdered nutrients cooked with melted snow, and gums haemorrhaging from scurvy. Temperatures plummeted as low as minus forty-five degrees and blizzards brought the risk of frostbite and snow blindness. How on earth they survived all of this without modern waterproof clothing is anyone's guess.

Dundee may not be universally known as the city that built *Discovery* but it is known to many as the city of jute, jam and journalism. There truly is no better way than alliteration, after all, to get people to remember things.

When Scotland joined the union with England in 1707 perhaps the greatest gift that came along with it was access to the global trade of Empire. Numerous places across the country benefited from this but, with its east-coast location on the sheltered Firth of Tay, Dundee was in a better position than most to cash in. What's more, during the nineteenth century Dundee was home to that large whaling fleet, bringing a regular supply of whale oil to the city's docks. With oil needed to soften fabric and a decent port needed for import and export, Dundee had no real rivals in its rise to becoming a so-called 'Juteopolis'.

Before I visited Dundee I had imagined that jute was a fabric of history, something ancient and long since surpassed by something far more efficient. Plastic, presumably. But in fact this inexpensive natural fibre is still used as a backing for carpets (by luxury brands Axminster and Wilton no less), lining for boots and shoes, furniture stuffing, roofing felt, damp courses and even cable coverings. At one time it would have been in almost every home in Britain – linoleum, or lino, is jute with a cement fixed over it.

It could even be described as hip: those hessian bags we all carry these days as a badge of our eco credentials are made from jute.

Intrigued as to why a fabric I thought was defunct is so entwined with Dundee's history, I leave the waterfront and weave my way into what was once an area replete with mills. At one time Dundee was home to some one hundred textile mills, and the area just to the west of the shopping centre retains a Victorian industrial feel in its cobbled streets. Although almost half of the city's mills have now been demolished, many are still used for housing and as warehouses. Some are even still used for textiles. And one is the city's museum of jute, aka the Verdant Works.

This mid-nineteenth-century solid stone mill is where I learned that I love jute. And not just because it has given us hessian, twill, tarpaulin and twine, housed the architects of more than one gold rush in tented camps and provided the sails for thousands of dream-soaked trips across the world's oceans in search of a better life. I found that I loved it because it gave local women a freedom they had never had before.

The jute industry created thousands of jobs, and many of them went to women. Women were cheaper to employ and as a result some three quarters of the jute workers were female. Dundee became known as 'She Town' and the *Dundee Yearbook* of 1888 shows the proportion of female householders in Dundee as the highest in Scotland. The resulting freedom meant that 'normal' female behaviour was different in Dundee than it was in other towns. Here women were like working-class men elsewhere: notorious for drinking and having a riotous old time.

But it could not last. Much of the pre-worked jute came from India, and as the industry there grew, the one in Scotland declined. Dundee simply could not compete with Calcutta, where workers were paid just £7 a week, instead of the £150 that was typical here at the time. Global trade, once the very thing that had made Dundee so successful, eventually killed its main industry. The city's recovery continues to this day.

Aside from jute, Dundee has numerous other claims to fame. Marmalade was invented here (that's the J for jam), and the gaming company that developed *Grand Theft Auto* started its life in the city. DC Thomson & Co was founded here in 1905 and has ever since produced some of Scotland's leading newspapers – there's that J for journalism – as well as introducing the world to Dennis the Menace and Desperate Dan through kids' comic books the *Beano* and the *Dandy*.

Dundee was also the first place where electric light was produced, more than forty years before Edison's infamous lamp.[18] I was determined to find the site of where it happened, Thistle Hall, a building that I knew to have been demolished but that I had read once stood on Seagate. Here in 1835 James Bowman Lindsay produced continuous electric light, something the world had quite literally never seen before. And yet he never registered or developed his invention. Although Edison is a name most schoolchildren know, pretty much nobody can tell you about Lindsay, and Dundee itself seems to have forgotten the man who should be one of their most famous sons.

Because for the life of me I could not find any sign of Thistle Hall. Thanks to the wonder that is Google Maps I confidently followed my phone to Seagate, but there I found pretty much nothing of note except the city's bus station. I walked the length of the street twice before I found myself standing, hands on hips in the manner of an exasperated cartoon character, looking towards a large, noisy junction. There is no suggestion at all that anything even remotely interesting has ever happened here. I wasn't expecting a shining plaque surrounded by a gaggle of electricity fans snapping pics, but I did think that some sort of marker would exist – even if tucked into a doorway somewhere – to extol the location of the start of something none of us could live without today.

Perhaps this is typical of Dundee, if not Scotland, though. This is not a country that shouts about its achievements. Sometimes I really wish that I could shake Scotland and tell it how phenomenal it is. But it would probably think I was taking the piss.

I might have fallen head over heels for Dundee but my next stop was to be the one city in Scotland I still struggle to get on with. Not because I don't like it as such, but because it has never quite grabbed me by the eyeballs or the heart and made me desperate to come back.

Perth was once Scotland's nominal capital (pre 1437, when Edinburgh officially took the title), and today it is home to plenty of 'oldest' this and that. But somehow none of it is all that exciting. St John's Kirk in the city centre is a pretty church and the city's oldest building, but it is dead as a doorpost on my visit. John Knox gave a sermon here in 1559 that kicked off a riot and started the country's Reformation. The riots are hard to imagine in Perth today, but the austere moral tone of the resulting Church of Scotland probably sat pretty well here.

What Perth is quite rightly famous for is Scone Palace. It was the site of the ancient Pictish capital, where Kenneth MacAlpin – often credited with being the very first King of the Scots – united two peoples (the Picts and the Gaels) under one crown in 843. This could be said to be the moment Scotland was born.

MacAlpin also brought the Stone of Destiny to Scone Palace. He installed it on Moot Hill and for centuries it remained there, the seat on which all Scottish kings were crowned. The stone was stolen, as we know, and so today it is a replica that sits atop the mound of Moot Hill, along with a panel that tells a compelling tale: that the hill was formed by lords carrying earth in their boots, literally bringing part of their lands here to Scone so that they could swear loyalty to the new king on their 'own land'. That some small part of all the lands of Scotland could be sitting here in a mixed-up heap beneath my feet is an idea that makes my senses spin. I stand for a few moments here, daydreaming of all the places I am about to discover.

CHAPTER FIVE

Into the Highlands

Grey can be the most beautiful colour. This was what I was beginning to realise as I pointed the car northwards and headed for the Highlands. As the sun dipped in the late afternoon, the sky darkened. Smoke-grey clouds sat densely above the darker, more charcoal grey of the mountains. Above them the sun shone through weakly, casting a wispy white-grey light. The landscape had become a palette of greys: it was the most serenely exquisite scene I had encountered on my journey around Scotland thus far. It reminded me of the faded black-and-white photographs of my grandparents' family albums.

This is the magic of the Highlands. A landscape that has inspired not just those who have written ballads and books about it, but also those who have fought for it, over centuries. There is an innate romance to the Highlands, a place with natural walls so sheer entire peoples and cultures can develop in splendid isolation. The Highlands are not quite like the rest of the country, and as Samuel Johnson remarks in his *A Journey to the Western Islands of Scotland*, the people are not quite the same as their Lowland counterparts:

Their rocks, he said, *secluded them from the rest of mankind.*

But this romance is not something I understood on my first visit, several years ago. Before I came here I had understood the Highlands to be some abstract concept, not quite a defined place. I had assumed it was empty, barren, a desolate landscape most people had left for the bright lights of the southern cities, or for new lives across oceans. I was wrong.

Shortly after leaving Perth I cross the Highland Boundary Fault. This line across Scotland runs from the island of Arran in the west to Stonehaven on the east coast, and it is far from an abstract concept. It is the dividing line between two different types of rock, and it definitively marks out what is Highland and what is not.

For my first stop in the Highlands I had booked a three-night stay in an apartment on Loch Tay, and I was giddy with excitement at the prospect of being able to unpack a few things and even do a load of washing. Living out of a suitcase is always hard and now that I was heading into hiking country it was about to get a whole lot tougher. Nobody wants their sweaty hiking socks knocking around the same airspace as their pyjamas, after all.

Loch Tay is just one of more than thirty-one thousand lochs that stretch across Scotland's sodden landscape, a glorious expanse of dark, still water that starts just outside my window in Kenmore and stretches for some fifteen miles south-west. I have chosen to stay here because it is within easy striking distance of two places I have always wanted to visit: Schiehallion and Rannoch Station.

Schiehallion is a mountain I have wanted to climb ever since I first saw her on a sunny day on Loch Rannoch. From that loch she is a perfect peak, a mountain that could be used as the emoji for one. She is also the perfect first Munro to climb, a relatively easy hike for anyone with map-reading and compass skills and the right gear.

A Munro is any Scottish mountain whose peak stands higher than three thousand feet (914.4 metres) above sea level. They were catalogued by Sir Hugh T. Munro in 1891 (hence the name), and ever since it has been the preserve of a particular sort of thick-sock-wearing hiker to 'bag' them all.

For me, though, hiking isn't about ticking off a list of mountains so you can boast about having completed some sort of challenge. It is about feeling our place in the world, as a physically small but hardy species that may have conquered nature but will never, ever tame it. It is about taking the mind, as well as the body, out of captivity. I have also always found hiking healing, and after a tough year of being buffeted by the strong winds of grief, I needed to know I could stand alone in a harsh landscape and conquer something by myself.

The car park for Schiehallion is just over three hundred metres above sea level, and so on setting out I find myself surrounded by heather and ferns. I shed a layer or two as the sun breaks through soft white clouds and pound my way uphill easily on a wide track that is stony but smooth underfoot. This, of course, is the easy part.

As the path works its way upwards steps begin to appear, as do some meaner-looking clouds. The path becomes darker and narrower, reminding me of the softly grainy chocolate biscuit cake I used to make with my mum as it crunches underfoot. Suddenly it disappears altogether and I am on my own in a boulder field.

"Dinnae worry, there's no right way," shouts a chipper voice somewhere away to my right.

"No, only lots of wrong ones," I reply.

"Aye, true enough," the voice comes back as a flash of bright Gore-Tex finally catches up with it, "but if you keep heading for that cairn it'll see you right."

Despite the man-versus-mountain maxim of Scottish hiking there are often signs to keep you on the right track, literally, and these cairns are one of them. They sit at the crest of each ridge, a pile of the same stones I am clambering over formed into a chunky cone shape similar to a trig point. My mind wanders this way and that as I pick my way through the boulders but my feet continue to head towards the cairn, and each one that follows – a relief when the clouds close in around the peak and hide her from view for a minute or two.

Walking up a ridge like this means facing the constant disappointment of the false summit, a crest in the side of the mountain that looks like it simply must be the top, until you reach it and see another ripple of mountain ahead of you. There are many of these on the way up Schiehallion but I am determined that I will reach the top, and as I am following a couple with a dog I feel confident that I am going the right way and am not entirely alone.

As it turns out, I am not even remotely alone. On a good-weather day in autumn Schiehallion is a popular place to be, and as I finally emerge onto the small, blustery plateau that really does turn out to be the top, I discover a dozen or so other walkers happily munching away on sandwiches and enjoying the view of Loch Rannoch. "Would you take our photo?" becomes the soundtrack of my time up here on the roof of the world, and I find myself swapping travel tales with a group of six Australians nearing the end of the Rob Roy Way. *If only I didn't have the car*, I catch myself thinking, the desire to strike out on a long-distance walk ever strong.

For now, I sit with my sandwiches and look out over Rannoch Moor. The landscape is greener than I had imagined, more verdant than it is barren. In Scotland the end of summer doesn't mean a burnt landscape as it does further south; here it is one of the greenest times, with no snow to obscure the colours. This is the first Munro I have climbed entirely alone and I am filled with a sense of accomplishment.

There is something romantic about a single-track road. Not the strip of tarmac itself, I mean, but the way they make you drive. You have to interact with other people when you are sharing a lane. There is no blithely pushing through on a single-track road;

somebody has to pull into a passing place for either of you to get about your journey. And so, you must learn to see cars as the people who are driving them, rather than as some sort of odd parasites that have a mind of their own.

In the Highlands your car is not a private space. You may even have to stop, wind down the window and talk to someone about how everyone is going to get past each other. And so I was not all that surprised to find myself flagged down by a woman with bright orange hair and manic outstretched arms on the road to Fortingall the next morning. A pair of cherry-red glasses slid down her nose towards me as she leaned into my window and asked a question that inspires dread in the heart of any Londoner: "Have you got a couple of minutes?"

My first thought is of surveys and clipboards, some sort of market research (stupid, of course), but then I spot the sheep.

"We're just moving our sheep across the road into the other field," she tells me, before launching into a story that seems to be several interwoven tales about the sheep's well-being. From the field her husband shouts something that is immediately lost in the breeze and she is off once again, gesticulating her thanks as I switch off my engine.

In the Highlands you wait when something like this happens. You sit and watch the sheep cross the road, or the farmer drive a herd of cows along to the next field, or BT fixing a roadside phone line from a cherry picker. If I had been in a rush (tending to a medical emergency, say), I could have said so and the sheep could probably have been coaxed back so I could get through. But I wasn't. Out here it is best to learn not to be.

I was driving to Fortingall to see a tree that is said to be the oldest in Europe, possibly the world. So it was unlikely to be moving any time soon. The Fortingall Yew is reputed to be five thousand years old. Of course, nobody can say for sure. But what an irresistible idea it is that this tree stood here three thousand years before Christ was born and several hundred years before anyone in Egypt thought to build a pyramid. It's seen entire civilisations come and go, empires rise and fall, and all manner of silly arguments over whose land is this, whose river is that. I find myself mesmerised for a while by the yew's thick tangle of trunks and branches. It is just impossible to reach back far enough into history to understand how long it has stood here without losing all sense of time and space. How small we really are. How little our pain is to the world. There is, I find, something oddly comforting about that. Ashes, always, to ashes.

A friend of mine comes from a small town near Glasgow but has lived in London for years. When I told her about my trip around her home country she gave me only one place not to miss. That place was Rannoch Moor. About nowhere else had I heard her speak with such reverence. She was almost breathless, lost for words in trying to describe just how awesome – in the truest, most original sense of that word – this landscape is.

And, frankly, I don't know if I can better her. Because what a place it is. During the last Ice Age this high plateau was covered by a vast ice sheet. As it retreated it scraped and grated the rocks, gouging lochs out of the landscape. One such loch is Loch Laidon, where I have chosen to take a walk.

It is one of those soggy days that Scotland does so wholeheartedly, especially in the west. Lumpen grey clouds hang overhead, heavy with the promise of rain, and at midday it still seems as if the day is struggling against the night. I have started, though, to think of a lighter shade of grey as the weather brightening up, and so I don my waterproofs, tug on a hat and head out from Rannoch Station.

At first the landscape around me seems so samey, almost barren. But then I start to notice the little things: the soft purple flowers, the red-and-white spotted mushrooms that look like an illustration in a children's fairy tale, the fact that the water bulges up from the ground and is almost at the level of the path.

This is a sodden landscape and it feels as if water is oozing up from every patch. Rannoch Moor is an area of breathtaking bog, and although there are trees along the loch little else is here to put down roots and knit the peat together. I have walked from a train station, complete with buildings and power lines, but out there is treacherous terrain – replete with tales of people falling into bogs up to their armpits, and worse. It is not a place to strike off into alone.

There is a silence, too, one that is almost haunting. I feel as if I can hear a creak in the air, like something unseen moving. It is like watching a horror movie, the bit where all goes quiet and you just know the killer is about to strike. The promised rain has been my companion for a while now but I notice the drops getting fatter and more insistent. Walking in Scotland may be all about dressing for the weather but it is also about knowing when the weather has beaten you. I retreat, bedraggled, to the station.

Immediately I am in another world. Rannoch Station may be surrounded by some of the most remote landscape in Scotland, but it is still on the Glasgow-to-Fort William railway line, and every half-hour or so a train chugs through on the West Highland Line. You can even get the sleeper directly from here to London. The station tea room is also the hub of the community, and as I pull open the door a warming cloud of hot air and chatter tumbles out to meet me. There isn't an empty table to be had.

This being the Highlands, I do something I never would in London: I approach a table of three people and four chairs and ask to share. Over pots of tea and plenty of "Pass the milk" we – all English – discuss what has brought us here and the fact that none of us is actually here either by or for a train. Through fogged windows I occasionally catch sight of a carriage or two but it is the homemade cakes that have my fullest attention.

This tea room is used by hikers aplenty, coming in to fill up their water bottles with peaty tap water the colour of Irn-Bru and to dry out after the rain. I comment to the woman on the till that it's a bit dreich today.

"Aye, but I prefer it like this; much more atmospheric," she says in that almost dreamy voice my friend back in London used. When I ask her if she's from here she says, "No, I'm fae just south of Glasgow. I moved here, met my husband and that was me, thirty years later. It's a hard place to leave." She's right, and I spend far more time here than I mean to.

The Grampian Mountains have been looking down at me from the north for several days. Home to a lengthy line-up of Britain's highests (mountain, ski resort, railway, restaurant), this mountain range is not only the loftiest but also the largest in Britain. It is a dizzying landscape of peaks that is, naturally, best explored on foot. But with winter starting to show its cards and my time running short I must make do with a quick visit.

I was most excited to take a ride on that highest railway. It is the Mountain Railway up Cairngorm Mountain and, constrained by my need to get to Ullapool by a certain date, my only choice if I want to ride on it is to head up there today. Unfortunately it is the sort of day that warm baths and log fires were invented for. Not to mention head-to-toe waterproofs, which I spend an increasingly exasperated few minutes battling with in my car.

So I am not in the best mood as I take a seat in the bright blue carriage and wait to be whisked up to some 1,100 metres above sea level. The eight-minute journey transports me into a cloud and deposits me at Britain's highest shop and restaurant. I peer out into the gloom, heading outside despite the cold to see if somehow the window was making that cloud appear thicker, but there isn't a scrap of blue sky to be seen. Nor a mountain. A board tells me that Ben Nevis can be seen on the horizon. I stare out disconsolately and wish I could hang around longer and wait for clearer weather.

Instead I content myself with buying a couple of postcards in that highest shop and posting them in the UK's highest postbox. At 1,097 metres above sea level, it tells me. One thing I love about the lack of mobile phone signal that plagues most of rural

Scotland is the way it has made me return to snail mail. Where before I might have sent a WhatsApp to a friend, now I send a colourful picture of a train, a mountain or a dolphin to the whole family – and, when I do have signal, receive pictures back of my friend's children holding them up with grinning faces and waving a cheery thank-you. It is heart-warming for a lonesome traveller, and a far better way of marking special travel moments than social media could ever be.

Also at the top of the funicular railway is a small exhibition, which tells me that this high plateau is more like the Arctic than the rest of Scotland. In some areas there is snow all year round, and in the winter of 2010 skiing here continued more or less uninterrupted from the 28th November to the 21st June. During this time the train track had to be dug out of the snow no fewer than four times. I do not remember hearing anything about this in London, where we were probably standing on platforms waiting for trains later cancelled due to a light dusting of powder, or the wrong kind of leaves.

CHAPTER SIX

Aberdeen and Inverness

I wasn't ready to leave the Cairngorms. I love the mountains and I could feel myself unwinding in their crisp, fresh air. So I decided to loop back on myself through the eastern half of the national park and head for the east coast from here instead, taking my time. Aberdeen could wait.

There is certainly plenty to see. The Cairngorms National Park is the largest in the UK and is twice the size of England's Lake District. To the untrained eye the landscape here seems barren, and as I drive across the plateau the slopes of heather on either side of the A93 are seemingly bare of all else. In its size and scale the landscape reminds me of a desert, with all the associated risks of perishing alone in the wilderness for making foolish decisions such as not filling up with petrol or striking off across the land on foot while inadequately prepared.

I have prepared for being in a wilderness and am happy to take it easy, pootling along the highway, enjoying the scenery. Ever since leaving Perth I have been seeing signs pegged to the trees asking me to slow down for red squirrels and as I enter Deeside I see my first one in the flesh, hopping across the road in a flash of ginger.

Deeside is where Highland tourism is generally considered to have been born. This was down to Queen Victoria and her husband Prince Albert, who fell head over heels for the Highlands and purchased their own estate here, Balmoral, in 1848. Victoria and Albert well and truly bought into the myth and mystique of the Highlands, a vision harking back to the romantic portrayal of this part of Scotland in the extraordinarily popular novels of – him again – Sir Walter Scott. Victoria referred to "the independent life we lead in the dear Highlands",[19] and royal life at Balmoral is said to have been very different from life in the other royal palaces – less restrictive, perhaps. Even the present Queen is said to favour Balmoral over her other homes.

But so-called Royal Deeside, despite its moniker, is about far more than just royal connections. This bucolic slice of Scotland, which follows the River Dee from the Grampians right down to Aberdeen, is positively packed with castles. Aberdeenshire, in fact, has more castles per acre than anywhere else in the UK,[20] and the signposted Castle Trail lays out a route that takes in nineteen of them.

I love a castle but even for me nineteen seems rather a lot, and besides, I need to push on to Aberdeen. So I pick just one: Crathes Castle. No extensive research led to this choice, it just happened to be on my route towards Aberdeen, but by chance it turned out to be an excellent pick, because it is quite incredibly intact.

Most of the Highlands' tower houses were destroyed, at least in part, by the savage reprisals visited on the area by the English after quashing the final Jacobite Rebellion of 1745. But not this one. Here I find a spiral staircase leading up to oak-panelled rooms and one of the most intricately painted ceilings I have ever seen. It is painted with verses from the Bible, the words filling each cross-beam overhead. Seeing me wide-eyed and clearly impressed, a guide I hadn't noticed enter the room interjects into my thoughts: "It was expected that people of a certain income would own a Bible," she says, "but the Burnett family went one step further." Quite a step.

It turns out that the Burnetts were zealous rule-followers, and that this is why their sixteenth-century home is still in such good nick today. "They kept their heads down and trod a middle line," the guide tells me. "One son joined the Jacobites, but he escaped and there were no reprisals." Luck was perhaps on their side. Or maybe survival is always more likely for those who sit on the fence.

It's a thoroughly pleasant drive along the Dee to Aberdeen, and I am struck once again by how beautiful Scotland is even in its quieter moments. Driving along a standard A road, the sort nobody has thought to officially designate a scenic route, I find that suddenly the view through my windscreen is truly breathtaking. Leaves so brightly yellow they are practically neon fall in clouds and flurries from the trees either side of the road, while the afternoon light shafts through their branches in shimmering silver and slices across the tarmac. I briefly wish that I had a passenger with me who could capture it in a photograph, then realise this is daft – some moments pass too quickly for a photograph, and are better held in the mind instead.

Before too long I am sucked into Aberdeen's ring road, jolted out of my poetic reverie by the mental energy needed to negotiate the narrow streets of the city centre in search of my hotel. I have chosen to stay near Union Street, a thoroughfare that is often said to be the grandest street in the country – even, just sometimes, by people in Edinburgh.

I head straight out to explore and find that the sun has won its battle with the clouds and is bouncing off the thick granite of the buildings that line this wide street. Once again Scotland is showing me that grey can be the most beautiful colour, the muted tone of the granite letting the delicate arches, rusticated stonework and the occasional pillar or turret shine through.

The Town House at the eastern, or seaward, end of Union Street stands tall over the pedestrianised cobbles of Castlegate and the Mercat Cross, the traditional heart of the city. Announcements were once made from the terrace at its top, including those that proclaimed each new king. In 1715, in the midst of one of the failed Jacobite Risings, James Francis Edward Stuart, aka Bonnie Prince Charlie, was declared king here. Significant support for the Jacobite cause was found around Aberdeen.

Today, though, Aberdeen seems pretty happy with the way things are, thank you very much. The city is a prosperous place and, depending on how you slice the statistics, could be said to be the country's richest city. It may have fewer millionaires than Glasgow,[21] but disposable income per person here is the highest in Scotland,[22] and some of the country's most expensive streets and postcodes are found within Aberdeen's city limits.

Also here is what might just be my favourite building in Scotland, Marischal College. This gargantuan granite beauty is said to be the second largest granite building in the world, and my goodness, is it impressive. I spend a captivated few minutes walking along the wide pavement in front of it, trying to cram as much of it as possible into my camera lens. It feels like the child London's Royal Courts of Justice and Houses of Parliament would have, and is fronted by a statue of Robert the Bruce on horseback. It's a triumphant statue in front of a triumphant building and, as the ex-university building is now the headquarters of Aberdeen City Council, reads like a statement of intent to the world. One that says Aberdeen is a place of consequence.

Much of Aberdeen's success in recent years has come from oil and gas. But the city has always been a trading port of significant wealth. You need only look at the names of the roads running off Union Street (Golden Square, Diamond Street, Silver Street) to see that money is in the city's DNA.

The harbour has long been Aberdeen's generator of wealth, and the Aberdeen Harbour Board is said to be the oldest recorded business in Britain.[23] The harbour remains the lifeblood of the city today, and I keep seeing it staring back at me as I walk around the city centre. At Castle Street I look right to cross the road and am almost dazzled by a vast white NorthLink ferry sitting at the end of the street. Overnight this will take people to the Northern Isles of Orkney and Shetland but for now it is just hanging out there, making Aberdeen look tiny.

Standing more or less next to it is the Maritime Museum. This is the best place to get a grip on the industry that has made Aberdeen Europe's oil capital, and its glass front is like a viewing gallery staring out over the harbour. Before my visit I knew next to nothing about the oil and gas industry; by the time I left I understood why Aberdeen was the perfect place for it.

In 1959 the North Sea was discovered to be hiding a vast energy source, when a huge gas field was found off the coast of Holland. Geologists believed that this must continue as far as Britain, and so the North Sea was divided up into one-hundred-square-mile segments and licences for exploration were issued by the British government. Britain struck oil in 1970 when the Forties Oil Field was found about 110 miles east of Aberdeen. The first North Sea oil was piped ashore in June 1975, and by 1977 there were seven companies with supply bases in Aberdeen Harbour.

Aberdeen was an obvious choice for the oil industry because it was close to the oilfields, but there was far more to the decision to base operations here than that. Aberdeen also offered twenty-four-hour access to new quays built by the Aberdeen Harbour Board, plenty of industrial and housing land, access to university-level research facilities, an airport, good road and rail links and – perhaps above all – a welcoming local government. Soon the world's biggest and busiest civilian heliport was here, ferrying workers to the oil rigs offshore, and Aberdeen had the highest wages in Scotland.[24] The effect on the city was immense. Panels in the museum tell me that in 1961, 39% of families living in Aberdeen had no private toilet. By 2012 the city had the highest rate of multimillionaires per hundred thousand in the UK, relegating London into second place.

What is shocking is how the UK has frittered this success away. The museum tells me that the UK's production capacity of oil and gas is the largest in the EU and the second largest in the EEA after Norway. That puts the UK in the top twenty producers of oil and gas worldwide. So where has all the money gone? There is so much focus on the Middle East and its wealth that stems from oil, but the UK as it stands today has the resources within its own shores to be self-sufficient. What has gone wrong?

The answer perhaps lies in Norway. When Norway discovered oil the government decided not to spend all of the money generated as it came in. Instead they set up a sovereign wealth fund, with the express aim of creating wealth in the long term. It is owned by the people of Norway and today is worth more than $1 trillion. Imagine how that sort of wealth could have helped the UK and Scotland in recent years.

Perhaps the UK will get a second chance. The museum's displays also discuss wind and wave power. One stat hits me hard, stating that: *The UK is the world leader in offshore wind energy generation, with as many offshore wind turbine generators already installed as the rest of the world put together.*

The rest of the world put together. That presumably means that we have more potential in the UK than anywhere else on the planet to keep the lights and the computers on with energy derived from the wind – something we have in abundance. And Scotland is the hub of it all. Perhaps it is time we stopped treating Scotland like England's poor, financially draining sibling.

My next stop is Dufftown. It is an instantly likeable town but to be honest I had been pretty keen on it before I even set foot in it. Because I love whisky – Scotch in particular – and Dufftown has the highest concentration of whisky distilleries in the country.

Dufftown is the ideal place for a whisky tour and I have booked a room at the guest house I'd been told I'd be able to find the most whiskies in one place: Tannochbrae. I find it on the main street, just beyond the chunky stone clock tower that stands sentry over the town's central crossroads. I have arrived on a Friday evening, with grand plans for a lively weekend break in Speyside. I envisaged the distilleries full of Scots sampling whiskies to take home, the local pub throwing up a ceilidh or some live folk music, and the whisky bar at Tannochbrae packed with knowledgeable drinkers I could swap tips with.

It turned out that I should have come on a weekday. With lots of distilleries closed at the weekends (Balvenie and Ballindalloch to name just two), there are very few people around on this dreich weekend evening. I retreat to the guest house whisky bar and find that I have it to myself.

Apart from James, that is; the owner and clearly a malt whisky connoisseur. The first question I ask him on my arrival is how many whiskies he has in the bar. "Close to four hundred at the moment, I think," he says. "We have the largest selection of single malts in Dufftown." Now there's a challenge.

Over a Balvenie 15 and a Tamdhu 10 we discuss the future of the whisky industry. "It's really booming," James tells me, running through a list of new distilleries opening this year and next. My head spins with all the whisky distilleries on my 'to-visit' list. Or perhaps just with the whisky.

The stats are even more head-spinning. Scottish whisky is a whopping £4 billion-a-year export industry. Some three quarters of this is made up of blends, but in 2016 the export value of single malts topped £1 billion for the first time. The international market is getting more discerning, more willing to spend on quality, and there is serious cash to be made. So serious, in fact, that Scotch is the largest net contributor to the UK's balance of trade and represents more than 20% of the UK's total food and drink exports.[25]

That the distilleries I spend my next few days visiting are slick affairs comes, then, as no surprise. First up is Glenfiddich, and first impressions are neat as a pin. A Saltire flutters in the breeze above a creamy-white wall, sandy-grey stone buildings sit squat beneath a darkly tiled pagoda, and a statue of a stag stands proudly at the entrance to the Malt Barn.

'Glen Fiddich' means 'Valley of the Deer' in Scottish Gaelic, and I cannot escape the stag logo anywhere. I take a seat close to the bar, backlit in yellow and gold to show off those iconic bottles, and decide I am going to spend considerably more on whisky than on lunch. There is a menu of whisky flights, you see, and I really want to see if I can tell the difference between a twelve-year-old and a twenty-one.

It turns out that I can (younger means less spicy, more fresh in this case), but only for about the first sip. Four drams before 1pm being what it is, I write copious notes about flavour which include words like 'toffee' and 'DELICIOUS', and happily swagger off to the shop to buy a bottle of the fifteen-year-old to take home.

One of Dufftown's other delights is the Whisky Line, or more officially the Keith and Dufftown Railway. I'm a sucker for a heritage train journey, and with no more open whisky distilleries in walking distance and a slightly tipsy air of spontaneity coming over me, I decide to take a trip out through the Speyside countryside by train for a closer look at the landscape.

Instantly I feel like I have returned to England. It is easy to assume that everywhere in the Highlands must be, well, high, but here in the north-east the landscape flattens out into rolling hills and barley fields. I sit back and let the soporific clack of the tracks beneath the carriage wheels lull me into a peaceful near-slumber. I am delighted just to sit and stare out of the window, letting my warm whisky fug lift as the minutes idly pass. As we travel through a timber yard all the folk working stop, lean on their tools and their timber offcuts, and wave. They look like the sort of cheery characters you normally only see in children's books, and I wave back with a massive smile, feeling as if I might be travelling on Thomas the Tank Engine. Further on, a couple of foxes gallop suddenly out from the woodland and run along between the lines ahead of us. At first they look back over their shoulders as if they know exactly what is happening and really don't care one hoot, but then they get spooked and dart off into the trees, presumably realising that being chased by a train never ends well.

I settle back into my seat and am just debating whether I should buy a snack or not – that whisky-to-lunch ratio not quite working out for me – when the train slides noisily but calmly to a stop a hundred metres or so short of a trio of sheep. All of a sudden the conductor appears, making her way towards the carriage door to step out and shoo the sheep away. The toot of the train's whistle seems to do the trick and the sheep turn to us with nonchalance and slowly move off the track. If I hadn't sobered up somewhat by this point I could be convinced that I had imagined it all.

The next day I am very soberly heading for a battlefield. Nowhere in Scotland has the atmosphere of Culloden. This windswept moor, with its long grasses, clumps of heather and boggy ground, was the site of the last full-scale battle ever to be fought on British soil. Close to 2,500 men died here on the 16th April 1746 and the ramifications of that day stretch right down through history, through the resulting Clearances and the desecration of the clan system, to the present day. The past is still very much felt here.

And so I am a little disappointed to find Culloden Moor bathed in sunshine. I had always imagined a visit to the battlefield taking place sombrely under leaden skies, but for my visit the skies were dazzling blue and dogs were frolicking in the grass. This is a solemn place, a war grave, and it is one that demands respect. I do not smile at the ruddy-cheeked woman letting her dog wee on the grass.

Instead I walk away from the crowds near the visitor centre and out onto the battle site. Here I find marker stones laid in the locations of mass graves, many of them inscribed with the name of the clan that fell here. That so many men were killed here in such a short and bloody battle is surely Scotland's greatest sadness.

The story that brings us all here, though, starts far earlier, back inside the museum and with the birth of a certain James, later to be known as Bonnie Prince Charlie. It's a complicated historical landscape to navigate but the museum is a well-balanced one, the stories of the Hanoverians and the Jacobites told on opposite sides of the same room, the events that led up to that fateful day in 1746 unpicked.

The strands that wove themselves together to lead to the Battle of Culloden are many and varied. There was the Catholic faith James VII was born into and which England couldn't stand to see on the throne, there was the French interest in a strong Scotland (and a weak England), and there was the disparity between the economic gains seen by the Lowlands post union with England and the hardship many lived under in the Highlands.

Although Culloden was in many ways a battle between England and Scotland, it is not possible to reduce this tragic battle to a war between two countries. More Scots fought on the Hanoverian side than on the Jacobite, for example, and there were Jacobite soldiers who came from Ireland, France and even England.

The fact remains, though, that without the Highland clansmen there could have been no Jacobite Rebellion at all. This is not a history book and a full assessment of the Jacobite cause would run to many hundreds of pages, but what cannot be disputed is that Culloden was an unmitigated disaster for the Highlands.

I had always thought of Culloden as the end of something, but in many ways it was more a beginning – of hundreds of men being hunted down and executed, and of countless families being cleared from their ancestral lands. The Duke of Cumberland installed an army in the Highlands, who spent the next few months burning communities to the ground and killing any supposed rebel they could get their hands on.

This was a project to destroy Gaelic culture. Both the plaid kilt and the Gaelic language were banned and many people were sold into slavery across the Atlantic, or transported to Australia and a life of hard labour. This brutal suppression earned the duke the title 'Butcher Cumberland', and his order that the Jacobites should be given "no quarter" meant that the Highlanders were treated like savages. In London the thirst for blood was intense and there were parties in the streets when news of Cumberland's victory reached the city. This was a terrible episode in Scotland's history and an extreme low point in relations between Scotland and England. I walk across the battlefield lost in thought and finding it hard to be proud to be English.

CHAPTER SEVEN

The Far North: Up to John o'Groats

It's a gorgeous day for my visit to Cromarty. The sun is streaming down from an almost resolutely clear blue sky and people are walking around rustling purposeless waterproof jackets under their arms, quite unsure of what to do with them. The sunny weather means that my trip out dolphin spotting with EcoVentures is full, the RIB (rigid inflatable boat) packed with twelve camera-toting tourists eager to meet the Moray Firth's dolphins.

"There are about two hundred dolphins living here," our captain, Sarah, tells us as she fires up the engine and unties the ropes. "They're the biggest bottlenose dolphins in the world. They can get up to four metres long." We are all just digesting this information and fiddling with the various straps on our lifejackets when Sarah shouts backwards, "Hold on tight, it might be a bit bumpy on the way out. We're heading directly into the wind." The woman next to me's knuckles fade from white to bone.

She is right to cling on. The ride out into the Cromarty Firth is like a rollercoaster, the RIB rearing up on top of the waves before crashing back down into the water. As we speed out to sea twelve faces break into childlike grins and we are splashed by the bracing North Sea until it drips from our eyebrows. I start not to care whether we see those dolphins or not and let out an undignified whoop.

There's a lot more to see in the Cromarty Firth than just dolphins. This sheltered inlet is home to a dozen or so oil rigs, sitting in ghostly silence just offshore. "When the North Sea is quiet or oil prices are low, the rigs get towed here and the firth becomes like a car park," Sarah says, as we sidle up to one of six massive yellow metal legs. "If you know your rigs, this one is famous. It's Hutton TLP. The owner pays something like £125,000 a year to keep it here."

The legs tower above us, each one like the funnel of a sunken ship, redundant and rusting away. This was the first tension-leg platform to be used in the North Sea[26] and it was built right here, across the water from Cromarty in Nigg. There were concerns that its relatively spindly legs wouldn't be enough to withstand the North Sea storms; I try to imagine a storm violent enough to topple a fifty-nine-foot-wide[27] (eighteen-metre-wide) column of steel. On such a sun-drenched day it's impossible, and besides, people are getting restless for those dolphins. The Cromarty Firth leads out into the Moray Firth, where we are most likely to see them, and as we speed on out to sea I pull my phone from beneath my jacket and start jabbing through the far-too-effective waterproof pouch I sensibly put it in, trying to get it to come to life.

Before I have much success, we stop abruptly. "Gannets," Sarah says. "A good sign." We bob in the water for a few minutes, each scanning hopefully for any movement that isn't a bird. We are running out of time and Sarah is starting to suggest that we might need to turn back soon. The tension mounts in the boat; dolphins are the whole point of this trip for most of the passengers and those white knuckles insist that we see at least one or two.

Suddenly there is a puff on the horizon, a noise so quiet it could have been drowned out by the smallest gust of wind. The adults in the boat try not to squeal with delight as two, then three, then five or six sleek grey backs arch through the waters towards us. I realise it is pointless to try and capture this – another Scottish moment that no photo could ever do justice to. Instead I fix my eyes on those dolphins, some three or four metres away and circling the boat as if checking out who has come to see them today. They slice through the water, halfway between us and the steep, tree-cloaked cliffs of the Black Isle. All is silent on board; nobody wants to return to Cromarty.

This is, of course, not to say that Cromarty isn't wonderful. It just doesn't tend to be the reason most people allocate a day or so to this part of eastern Scotland. I didn't really mean to stay in Cromarty myself. The village is one of those places that a lot of people visit already planning to leave – most of them on Sarah's boat trip – and I hadn't planned to stick around.

But there was something about the place. It started in the bakery, an unassuming wee shop that I had been told, several times, makes the best oatcakes in these parts. They also make excellent pies, and do a fine line in selling the village to passing pastry lovers to boot. The guy on the till is very keen to tell me about the great internet coverage they get here. "There wouldn't be a web design business here without it," he tells me proudly, gesturing along the street as I munch on my pie. "They come in for cakes all the time." He also tells me about the local craft ale company, the Cromarty Arts Trust who put on festivals and events in the old brewery, and the local seafood restaurant I could go to for dinner. I am tempted into an overnight stay. After all, it sounds like I'll even be able to watch Netflix.

I am also tempted into a pre-dinner stroll around the village. There are plenty of people doing the same thing, and as I say hello to the umpteenth person I realise I am guilty of always assuming small, rural places to be stagnant. I imagine their residents pulling out of their driveways as the sun rises, off to the big smoke and the job that pays for the chance to live somewhere nobody much will bother them.

I really should know better, coming from Wiltshire. But perhaps London has dulled my peripheral vision. There is, after all, a world out there, away from the suburbs and flight paths, where people are doing incredible, creative things in small communities. How smug of me to think the action only happens in London, or perhaps Edinburgh, Glasgow, and Dundee at a stretch.

That said, Cromarty did enter economic decline back in the nineteenth century but this has only enhanced its attractiveness. Here decline has meant preservation. Rather than being modernised for late-nineteenth-century industry, buildings were left alone to wait for better times and this ancient fishing village is today one of the best preserved in the UK.

It is also, apparently, where the great Ian Rankin begins his books. "When he's here he'll walk past the window about half past eight to get his paper," they tell me at Sydney House B&B when I check in for the night. "And he's often in the pub drinking the local beer." I decide I must find time for a pint later on.

First, I have more exploring to do. Cromarty is on the Black Isle, which is perhaps the worst-named place in Scotland. It isn't an island, for a start, and it certainly isn't black. And what an off-putting name for a place that is in fact home to charming fishing villages, fairytale woodland walks through birches and rowans to waterfalls, and some of the best land-based dolphin spotting in Europe.

You don't need to head out on a boat to see the bottlenose dolphins here. At Chanonry Point near the village of Rosemarkie, the peninsula slopes out into the Moray Firth in a narrow spit of land that channels the North Sea through a smallish gap. With less space to swim, the dolphins are pushed closer to shore and so sightings are much more likely here than pretty much anywhere else in Scotland. There's a lovely beach here too, replete with joggers and dog walkers on this balmy evening, as well as a campsite that was doing big business, with dozens of vans parked up along the back of the sands. From Chanonry Point itself you can look north-eastwards out to sea for those dolphins, or you can look south-west, straight down the Great Glen.

This was the view I chose to focus on, trying to pick out the great hulk of Ben Nevis, which I knew to be standing at the glen's far end. 'The Ben', as many people call it, is the tallest mountain in the British Isles, at 1,345 metres, but I am still amazed that there is even an outside chance that I would be able to see it from some eighty-five miles north.

To be fair, I am not certain that I can. For the purposes of being able to head to the pub in search of Rankin instead of continuing to try and ascertain exactly what I'm looking at, I decide that the bulky peak looming on the horizon is a likely enough shape to be the Ben and retreat to my car.

I don't find Rankin in Cromarty, but I do find one somewhat old-school form of transport; a tiny ferry that only takes two cars – or just one if it's particularly large. I love to travel on anything like this and so the next day I head down to the banks of the Cromarty Firth.

I am only heading to the next jut of land immediately to my north but this strip of water sits between me and my destination. The ferry from here to Nigg can save me an hour's drive back down the peninsula to the Cromarty Bridge. Unfortunately, the water level is extremely low, which turns out to be a problem.

The Cromarty ferry is the sort of wait-and-see-what-happens local infrastructure that I love. This is not a ferry service to rely on. Not because it isn't well run and efficient, but because sometimes the weather, or the tidal conditions, get in the way. And this was one of those days.

I wait at the pier with a geologist from down south and his

bike. A teeny café in what looks to be a shed is serving up the best coffee I've had in days and several local people are milling about having a blether with Sophie the barista. I mention that Shirley from the B&B has told me how good the coffee is here. "Oh yes, they're in here all the time," Sophie tells me. "Most people coming in aren't waiting for the ferry."

I, though, am, and am starting to wonder what's going on. It is not the Highlands way to hassle someone about when this or that method of transport might be able to run, or to stand around tutting and pointedly looking at your watch. Here a timetable that says 'every thirty minutes' is more a guide than a promise and I am in no way surprised when Sophie's response to my supposition that the ferry might be on its way soon is to look out the window and say, "Aye, it looks like he's over the other side at the moment but I'm sure he won't be long."

The geologist and I sip coffee and talk about the gold rush that started here with the discovery of a nugget in Helmsdale in the early nineteenth century. The ferry still doesn't move. We discuss how far we would have to go around to get further north today without the ferry and how long it might take us with the roadworks on the A9. Still the ferry doesn't move.

Eventually I call the ferry operator, and ask if he might be sailing soon. "Is it you waiting at the pier?" he asks me. "Thing is, the water level's too low. It's not high enough to drive the car on. But it's getting higher. It should be about half an hour."

Satisfied that things are working out and that I won't have to drive around the entirety of the Black Isle, I settle in for another coffee. But still the ferry doesn't move. Half an hour later the ferry operator phones me back. He is very apologetic but says it will be another half-hour. I find myself apologising to him that I won't be able to wait and asking him if he'd like me to pass on the message that it might be a while yet. I am turning into a Highlander.

My transformation appears to be complete that evening, at the home of a friend of mine, David, who is the chair of the North Highland Initiative. That day I have been severely held up by the A9, which qualifies me to discuss at length the ins and outs of this terrible road.

The A9 is the main road from the Highlands to Scotland's Central Belt. It runs from Dunblane through Stirling, Perth and Inverness to Scrabster Harbour on the north coast. This means that it links three of Scotland's seven cities with the gateway to the Northern Isles as well as the motorways for Edinburgh and Glasgow. That's a pretty important road. And yet in many places it is just one single carriageway wide.

The A9 has a reputation for being the most dangerous road in the country. This is mostly down to driver behaviour, and a major factor in that is the inability to overtake. Impatience doesn't mix well with Highland geography – there are plenty of blind bends here. There is much griping about there being space for a dual carriageway all the way, but the money has to come from somewhere.

Perhaps some of it can come from tourism. In 2015 a new touring route launched around the far north of Scotland. This is the North Coast 500, and it was created by the North Highland Initiative. The idea is to grow tourism in the region, a region that David tells me is "about the size of Wales".

This is a fragile area, and one that struggles to hang on to its population, a population that is less than 1% that of Wales. I hear of 'young people' heading to university or off on their travels, never to return, and communities are losing their banks, their local shops, their pubs.

But they will never lose their beauty, and this is what brings people – in their thousands, no less – to the North Coast 500. Not for the first time on my journey, a map is being spread out on a kitchen table. David and his friends are telling me about all the places I must not miss. No country I have ever been to lacks people who are proud of their country, but Scotland really is something else. Here everyone seems eager to share their favourite spots, and debates over which beach or seafood shack or waterfall is best can go on for hours.

Hopefully this desire to show visitors the secret spots will spread the tourist traffic out around the Highlands, but there is some concern about the huge increase in numbers that has been seen since the route was launched. About a quarter of people driving the route do it in a motorhome or camper van, and traffic has increased by around 10% along the route.[28]

As there always is with something new and different, there has been plenty of grumbling. When I wrote an article for the *Times* newspaper about the route, a reader wrote to me to complain that he could no longer stay at his favourite hotel because too many other people were booking it. This struck me as rather unfair. The hotel needs guests to survive, after all, and the Highlands themselves could be said to be no different.

I had always associated the Highland Clearances more with the western glens and the Hebrides than with Scotland's east. But this bitter period in Scotland's history began to haunt my travels almost immediately after passing the Cromarty Firth.

Heading north it felt at first as if I was not in the Highlands at all, the landscape a largely flat expanse of agricultural fields, many of them waving with the barley that will one day make it into my whisky glass. At Dunrobin Castle, in fact, you could almost be in France, its smooth grey stone walls reaching up to lofty spires capped with creamy tiles. It was designed in part by Sir Charles Barry, its formal gardens modelled on Versailles.

But Dunrobin Castle "makes Scottish people feel sick," one friend had told me. This is because it is the seat of the Sutherlands, a family who were at the helm of some of the most brutal and mercenary of the Clearances. In the early nineteenth century thousands of people were forcibly evicted from their land across Sutherland to make way for more lucrative large-scale sheep farming. Family homes were burned to the ground, children were made homeless, and livelihoods, in the most literal sense imaginable, were lost. It would not be overly dramatic to say that the first Duke of Sutherland killed many hundreds of people – by taking from them the means to feed their families. Many moved to the coast to begin lives as fishermen; many others were forced to emigrate.

You would not glean any of this from a tour of the castle, though. The Clearances are hardly a shining example of benevolent aristocracy after all, and so the displays focus instead on the fact that Queen Victoria once came to stay, and that during the First World War this was a naval hospital. I walk from room to room on the tartan carpets and wonder why we all seem to be so fascinated with people with money. In the dining room I overhear a woman say to her husband, "Fish before soup, do you think?" while looking quizzically at the way the cutlery is laid on the table. The level of detail they are looking at perhaps explains how some people manage to spend a full day touring these grand old houses. I am in and out in under an hour.

I am more interested in a stone figure atop a nearby hill. This is surely Scotland's most contentious statue, a memorial to the notorious first duke. It stands on Beinn a'Bhragaidh above the village of Golspie, a twenty-three-metre pedestal topped with a seven-metre George Granville Leveson-Gower in stone. It can be seen from many miles away.

It would be hard to find a figure more hated in local history. And so, unsurprisingly, the statue has been the target of vandalism and destruction consistently for many years. In 2010 the statue was spray-painted with the word 'monster', it has been almost toppled by the removal of sandstone bricks in its plinth, and it was hung with a Yes banner in 2014 by the pro-independence group – and brilliantly named – The Hills Have Ayes. It is surely time that the stone duke be evicted from his Highland home. Much of the Highlands is still suffering from the effects of the Clearances he precipitated, the most obvious of which is the lack of population. I find myself driving for mile after mile without passing a house, let alone a village, and as I scan the landscape for signs of human habitation, I spot the shells of former homes and farms littered across the landscape.

But there is hope. The Highlands are a truly beautiful place to make a life, and in our connected twenty-first-century world it has never been easier to run a business here. I find a fine example of this at the River Bothy, a few miles up the coast at Berriedale in Caithness. This was one of the places David had resolutely circled on my map, and since it sits right on the North Coast 500 it is an easy place to pull off the road.

It is no accident, of course, that it is here. "We opened because of the NC500," the woman busily clearing tables post lunch rush tells me. "It's going really well. We plan to expand into the space next door next year."

I am not surprised the bothy is doing so well; the sheer amount of cake and biscuits arranged across the counter would put many much larger city-based businesses to shame. There are cheesecakes and eclairs and shortbreads and scones. Everything is freshly made and beautifully presented. It is the sort of counter you imagine hoovering up with a big cakey smile on your face and chocolate cream smeared across your chin.

My excuse for having cake for lunch is the Whaligoe Steps, a plunging staircase that leads from the top of the cliffs down to a tiny harbour that was once an integral part of a booming herring-fishing industry. All the way up the east coast I find these stone-carved harbours, most of them now sitting sadly abandoned and unloved. There are plans afoot to get the local council to lease these harbours back to the communities so they can be used again, but for now the only one really worth visiting is Whaligoe, where I can test my leg muscles on a descent that may not rival a Munro in length but certainly does in steepness.

It is a difficult place to find. I see it marked on my North Coast 500 map a few miles short of Wick but there is no brown sign and, coming from the south, no obvious parking. I slow down to the sort of speed a tractor would find infuriating as my satnav tells me I have reached my destination, but before I spot a turning to the right I have sailed past and am heading for the outskirts of Wick. This is the dreaded A9, and as well as being narrow and lacking in straight enough sections for overtaking, it is severely under-provisioned with turning places. There is simply nowhere to pull off the road and so I drive further and further away from where I want to be, with more and more irritation. "These had better be some bloody interesting steps," I curse.

Finally I manage to turn around and approaching from the north there is a fairly obvious turn-off, though still no signpost. Fortunately the Whaligoe Café has put out a banner on the roadside; there is no other hint that this strip of tiny houses might be Whaligoe. The café is closed, a wizened man in dark green wellies is stomping up and down the pavement, and *RESIDENTS ONLY* is daubed across part of the car park in white paint. It doesn't feel very welcoming. There is a fairly obvious path running past the café, though, and some of the car park is free from white paint so I decide this must be it. I walk off towards the cliffs; the man in the dark green wellies doesn't bother me.

Well, it was all worth it. Because the Whaligoe Steps are marvellous. Chunks of Caithness flagstone are laid in more or less uniform steps straight down the cliff edge. Tufts of grass spring from the flagstone wall to one side; on the other sheer rock rears up, daring you to find a handhold. The steps weave down for several hundred metres to a flattish expanse of grass and rock, beyond which a steely, almost sapphire, sea is lulled into submission by the towering cliffs that surround it. Nobody else is in sight. Anywhere else in Britain there would be a large car park, coach parties and an ice-cream van; here in the far, far north of Scotland, somehow even the North Coast 500 isn't bringing more than a handful of visitors.

The plentiful Caithness flagstone is the reason so many harbours were constructed up this coast. It breaks naturally into panels when quarried, which makes it perfect for paving. Walk in New York City, in fact, and you're almost certain to be stepping on Caithness stone. Knowing the raw materials were already here in abundance, in 1790 Thomas Telford was dispatched to this coastline by the British Fisheries Society. His task was to identify the most suitable bay to develop for the herring industry. He chose Wick.

I could have wept for Wick. Because what a disconsolate place it is today. The town couldn't even seem to rustle up the smarts to charge for parking and so, having set my satnav to bring me to Ebenezer Place, I was able to park at the roadside without paying a penny. Had I arrived in a campervan the size of my house I still could have parked here for nothing, such was the expanse of empty tarmac.

I had set my course for Ebenezer Place because it is Wick's most famous street, the so-called shortest street in the world. It is impossible to find a write-up of the town that doesn't trumpet this *Guinness Book of World Records* wonder, and so I had in my mind a sort of pocket-sized Diagon Alley, probably very narrow, almost certainly cobbled.

I am sorely disappointed. Because Ebenezer Place is in fact the corner of Mackays Hotel, with a street sign bolted to the side of it. This side is the sloped edge of a roundabout, complete with cheap metal railings and diamond-shaped yellow hatching beyond. It is barely over two metres long. It is absolutely not a street.

Sadly, this set the tone for my time in Wick. This was once the so-called herring capital of Europe but today the harbour sits in near-silence, the odd sail thwapping against a mast in the breeze. For some reason Wick seems to have decided to reinvent itself as the budget home furnishings capital of northern Scotland instead, and as I walk along the empty streets I count four largely untroubled furniture and homewares stores. Signs touted sales and discounts, while inexplicable items (plastic buckets, a collection of lurid children's fishing nets) had been cast out into the street as an enticement to enter. Nobody was around to.

During the nineteenth century this northernmost part of Scotland was world-renowned. A fleet of more than a thousand herring boats sailed out from here daily and the catch of the day – the 'silver darlings', as the herrings were named – brought not just money but people, a great influx of young, work-ready blood and shrewd business sense. Many of them, though, were migrants. They weren't putting down roots in the town, or building families here. They were here to work the herring season, and would follow the great catches down the coast to England as the silver darlings, and with them the money, moved on.

Today they have moved on permanently and Wick is now home to only around seven thousand people. The population is decreasing, slowly but surely. The town centre is oversupplied with not just furniture shops but boarded-up buildings. For a town that appears to be so excited by home furnishings, there is an awful lot of peeling paint. On the main street I spot a *NO BALL GAMES* sign nailed to the wall and the nicest building I can find is a desultory Wetherspoons, lazily peddling cheap booze to anyone who still has the money for it. I really could have wept for the place.

Perhaps the oddest thing about Wick is its lack of an outdoors store. This is the most significant town for miles around, and that makes it the only shopping opportunity I have had for days. Had I needed more walking socks, a replacement compass or a better coat, I would have been denied the opportunity to spend a reasonably large sum of cash in Wick.

And of course I am not the only one. I am smack bang on the North Coast 500 here and yet my only real chance to spend any money (unless I really wanted to make a bet or grab a Chinese takeaway) was at the out-of-town Tesco I stopped at for petrol.

In need of a few provisions I head into the main store and am confronted with a high street bent and bowed into a warehouse. This cavernous, brightly lit shed is selling everything from bras to egg cups, carrots to nappies. I could load up a trolley with everything I could possibly need here and there would be no reason to go into town at all. Suddenly the reason Wick is deserted is clear.

So please, people of Wick, open a business. Open lots of businesses. Open an outdoors store, a place to buy food that isn't a supermarket, a café with dreamy hot chocolate and homemade cakes. Reach out and grab those people, coming in their thousands to travel the NC500, and make them stop in your town rather than at your Tesco. After all, you're better than John o'Groats.

Ah yes, John o'Groats. A place of such mystique that everyone travelling up this way is either heading there or has just been there. This is a natural meeting point on the NC500 because it is, very roughly, halfway, and because almost everyone stops here, and not just for a few minutes but generally overnight.

Because John o'Groats is miles from anywhere else worth stopping at, it has become worth stopping at itself. Except that it really isn't. Because, I discover, John o'Groats is not the northernmost point of the British mainland. Neither is it the most north-easterly. It isn't even at one end of the longest straight line you can travel in Britain without crossing salt water.

What John o'Groats is is an opportunist. This is a village that has decided it would like to be the end point, the full stop at the very top of Britain, and so has just started doing it. Fake it until you make it. Except that now young John has indeed made it, he doesn't seem very happy about it. Like a moody teenager who would really rather not get out of bed, John o'Groats really can't be bothered to offer anything approaching service, or value for the time spent here.

The place had already irritated me before my arrival, my

accommodation having called me at least twice to confirm my booking and then leaving a complicated email of instructions on how to access my bed for the night. This was a hotel without the hospitality. A key box rather than a smiling person is at the door to greet me, and the restaurant is shut up and sitting in darkness at 6pm even though every sign I found (as well as the website) quite clearly said it would be open until 7pm. None of it feels very Scottish at all and I find myself reeling at the loss of the Highland hospitality and general desire for a chat I have become so used to.

I am staying right on the waterfront, which is surely precisely where everyone thinking they are to spend the night at the northernmost reach of land would expect to. And yet I have to go inland a quarter of a mile or so to find dinner. What a wasted opportunity for the village to have somewhere serving local seafood on the waterfront, I think, as I walk with my back to a lovely view over the North Sea to Orkney.

Fortunately the pub in John o'Groats is OK bordering on good. Although the dining room hasn't quite been dragged from the 1970s just yet, there is a pleasant view of sheep in the field inland from the window, and proper pies on the menu. I've had quite enough of cheap-as-chips local lobster and lovely sea views anyway, I try to tell myself. And the reason John o'Groats seems quite so unwelcoming is that everywhere else in Scotland I have been has been so entirely the opposite.

Since the pub is the only place to eat for miles around, it is packed and I am delighted to end up sharing my table with two English couples, each one travelling the NC500 in a different direction. Since roughly half of people do it clockwise and half anticlockwise this is to be expected, and we talk at length about whether either approach is better than the other, dancing around anything positive we might have to say about the way we are doing it lest we upset those going the other way. This is, of course, what it is to be English.

For me, though – and I can say this now, being out of earshot of my clockwise-travelling friends – the route is far better done anticlockwise. Starting in Inverness, it is the east coast up to John o'Groats that is the easiest section to do speedily. After John o'Groats the reasons to stop increase exponentially, the landscape begins to rumple upwards into mountains again and the Western Isles hove into view. I had allowed more time for this section because it is, simply, spectacular. I couldn't wait to get started.

CHAPTER EIGHT

The North-West Coast

I had always assumed that the famous signpost at John o'Groats marked Britain's northernmost point, and I have been thrown off course by the realisation that the true northernmost point of Great Britain is in fact at Dunnet Head, some twelve or so miles west. Keen to stand in the spot that would make me the northernmost person on the island for a moment or two, I drive here the next morning, striking out onto the chunky, thumb-like peninsula and heading straight for the sea.

A few people have chosen to walk out here, but since the landscape is so wet they have had to stick to the road, which seems to defeat the point somewhat. This is a nature reserve, bought recently by the RSPB (Royal Society for the Protection of Birds), but with cars and campers zipping up and down the tarmac, there is too much disturbance close to the road to see very much. Sometimes it really isn't better to walk, I decided; a thought which was confirmed on my return journey when I passed the same pairs of walkers still slogging along the roadside.

Dunnet Head is well worth the diversion. This is a handsome

spot, a jade-and-russet landscape sodden with puddled lakes that ends abruptly at some of the highest, sheerest sea cliffs in Britain. The lighthouse, in brilliant white, is the northernmost building on mainland Scottish soil, and there's a sign – reminiscent of an ancient standing stone – just before it that states that this is *the most northerly point of mainland Britain*. It would be gorgeous even if it weren't for the scattered land mass of the Orkney Islands breaking up the otherwise blue horizon.

I can understand why the Queen Mother was such a fan of this coast. She fell in love with the area so much, in fact, that she bought the only home she ever truly owned, just a few miles along the road from Dunnet Head at the Castle of Mey. My guide for the obligatory tour tells our small cluster of twelve that the Queen Mother wasn't confident in her purchase. Not because she didn't love the castle, but because its sixteenth-century bulk required a lot of restoration. "But then Churchill said, 'If you like it, girl, go for it', and that was that," we are told. What an incentive.

What is different about the Castle of Mey is that it feels like a home, not a stately home. In the hall are the Queen Mother's wellies (size five), on top of the TV are *Dad's Army* videos, and I spot several books by Dick Francis, apparently the Queen Mother's favourite author. On the table in the living room is an Easter card from Prince Edward, and on top of a tapestry sits a cuddly Nessie, put there by the royal children as part of a game some years ago.

This is a lived-in castle, and Prince Charles still stays here once a year in August. Sadly, us commoners are not allowed to see the rooms he uses. "There are two bedrooms upstairs done up posh," the guide tells us. "We presume that's where they sleep." We do get to see the dining room, though, where the Queen Mother entertained every single evening, even after she passed her hundredth birthday. "She always took the guests outside to see the sunset, and nobody ever went home before midnight." No wonder she was so well loved, and that the UK practically stopped in its tracks when she died in 2002.

The Queen Mother loved gin – her first alcoholic drink of the day, always at noon, was a gin and Dubonnet – and so it is fitting that just a few miles from the castle one of Scotland's best gins is distilled. This is Rock Rose, made with Caithness botanicals by Dunnet Bay Distillery. Gin has become something of an enigma in Britain, with all sorts of closely guarded secrets about this botanical or that, and I am somewhat sceptical about all the chat around brands of tonic and slices of fruit.

But there is, refreshingly, no nonsense at Dunnet Bay. There is a wee shop here – more a kitchen sideboard packed with gin – but nobody tries to tell me how I should drink the gins on offer and I happily sip from a plastic shot glass of Rock Rose Original as I decide which bottles would make the best Christmas presents. There are seasonal gins, one for each of spring, summer, autumn and winter, and I leave with a boxload – the perils of having my own car and therefore no luggage allowance to stick to. Still, I'll be popular this Christmas.

I have been missing the high landscape I have always – quite naturally, I think – associated with the Highlands, and so I am delighted to be driving westwards, towards the more dramatic end of Scotland's northern coast. There is little to stop for along here, and with Orkney now too far behind me to liven up the horizon with a few dramatic lumps, I am keen to get some miles under my wheels.

For an hour or so I just point the bonnet west, my mind slipping between indeterminate thoughts. Then, just before Bettyhill, two lumps appear tantalisingly on the horizon. These seem to mark my entry into the north-west corner of Scotland, a landscape of supreme peaks, inlets like gashes made with a plunging knife, and roads that swing around corners so steeply that first gear and a gritting of the teeth are required.

This is the part of Scotland that burns the soul. If you love it, as I do, those mountains don't just smack you in the eye as you turn a corner near Tongue or make a sharp turn towards Ben Hope; they wallop you in the chest and take a hold of your heart. This can be a harsh landscape but it is one that rewards anyone who takes the time to truly discover it.

One of the best rewards in life, though, is, of course, chocolate. And above all else he recommended, David had impressed on me that I must, must, must visit the chocolate producer Cocoa Mountain. Well, now it is my turn to impress the same thing upon you. Because if you are anywhere within even the vainest hope's distance of fitting in a stop here, then you absolutely have to call in.

That Cocoa Mountain is here seems so unlikely at first. You are in Durness, for a start, the most north-westerly village in mainland Britain and by most measures the most remote to boot. But then you come across a craft village. There are art galleries here, as well as ceramicists and woodworkers, and in the midst of it all, just about the best chocolatier in Scotland.

Cocoa Mountain is primarily a café and so I take a seat at a table with a cracker of a view of the mountains and start to narrow down the choices in front of me. There are dozens of chocolates sitting in neat, cubed rows behind glass at the counter, and a hot chocolate comes with two on the side. There are champagne truffles, strawberry with black pepper, and peppermint fondants, not to mention whisky chocolates and a Turkish delight. Two was never going to be enough.

My afternoon passes in sugar-coated bliss. I order a hot chocolate and let's not say exactly how many of those chocolates, and sit there happily smearing chocolate all over my face, the napkin bowl, my phone and everywhere else my fingers come anywhere near. I practically bounce out of the place and back into the car.

Durness is also known for its fabulous beaches – and for a cave with the most wonderful name. Smoo Cave has the largest entrance of any sea cave in Britain, a gaping hole above a slender river that runs out between jagged cliffs to the ocean. Standing at its entrance I am closer to Bergen in Norway than I am to London, and the area's Norse heritage is obvious in that name: 'Smoo' comes from 'smúga', which means 'cave' in Norse.

There is a karst cave at the very back of Smoo, carved into the limestone over millennia and long used as a shelter. There is much evidence of past life here, from the nails and rivets discarded by those doing boat repairs, to the fish bones and shells left here by hunter-gatherers, perhaps as many as seven thousand years ago.

You have to do a tour to see the interior cave, and I have lingered so long in sugary oblivion that I have missed today's hours. Fortunately, the first chamber is free to enter and reached by a wooden boardwalk. Once out of the sunlight I can see the true colour of the fresh water, a rusty, peaty brown, and as I step further inside a roaring noise fills the cavern around me. A sign that looks like it could have been printed in somebody's kitchen and simply says *No!* has been attached to a wooden gate on the viewing platform. I peer over the edge and see a ladder down into water as frothed up as the head of a just-poured pint of beer. I find myself recoiling with trepidation in my chest. I doubt anyone would survive a swim down there.

About fifteen metres away from where I'm standing a torrent of water as white as ice is gushing into a dark pool. It is far more water than I had imagined and a much more dramatic spectacle than I had expected to see. This is the sort of cave that down south would require plenty of coach parking and a ticketed entry system. Up here in the far north of Scotland, signage is so limited that I am asked by an Italian tourist back at the roadside – in the car park for the cave, no less – where the cave is.

Back on the main road, it's a few miles further to Kinlochbervie, a place that comes as quite a surprise. I have been used to finding little more than a smattering of homes and outhouses – generally whitewashed and usually cottage-sized – in each village or hamlet I've been to, but pulling around the final corner before Kinlochbervie I am suddenly staring at a large fishing port. There are warehouses lined up along the harbourside, a sturdy red-hulled fishing vessel sitting in the waters, and a pair of vast trucks parked up ready to haul off the day's catch.

I turn into the car park of the Kinlochbervie Hotel to find a hive of activity. In the hallway the carpet is rolled into a fat cigar across the doorway and there is much kerfuffle going on beyond. The owner slightly breathlessly bustles up to the door to welcome me, apologising with what seems like every second word.

After I assure her that I really don't mind her carpet-free hallway, she relaxes and slips into typically warm Highland oversharing. "We're usually very quiet this time of year so this is when we do our upgrades," she tells me, "but the warehouse down at the harbour is being refrigerated over the winter so the workers are staying here. It's usually such a worry but we should have a good winter this year."

This can be the curse of Scotland. Anybody in England whom I tell I am visiting Scotland any time between about October and May will exclaim, "But what about the weather?" It is as if Scotland is somehow cut off during the colder months, a snow-cloaked, barren wasteland that must sit and wait for the big thaw come spring before expecting anyone to visit.

I've always thought that this is very unfair. England is hardly the Caribbean by comparison after all, and there are plenty of fine, clear days during the Scottish winter when the sky is bluer than in any summer haze and the hills' snowy caps glisten like an Alpine ski resort. A day on which it rains non-stop is about as common (or as rare, in fact) as it is in England, and there have been plenty of occasions on my travels when I have enjoyed warmer temperatures in the Highlands than I would have at home.

The following day was a bright but cloudy early-winter day. The lack of rain was a relief because I was setting out to walk to a beach I had always wanted to visit – a walk of some four miles. Sandwood Bay is the reason most tourists stop in Kinlochbervie. It is just a few miles from the hotel to Blairmore car park, the trailhead, and here I find a trio of campervans, several cars and a welcome block of toilets.

The walk may be long but the track is well defined and impossible to lose – pretty much all else here is bog. As I hike, squally showers pass overhead and I spend my time putting on my jacket, taking off my jacket and wondering whether I should put on or take off my jacket. It is a diverting enough stream of thought that I eat up the miles very quickly, buffeted along by a breeze at my back and the desire to catch up with any walker I see on the horizon up ahead. I am keen to get the sands to myself, even if only for a few minutes, and I am happy when I note that at least a dozen people have passed me on their way out. I find myself wondering, and then calculating, just how many cars there were in that car park.

Plenty of people find Scotland's bogland hard to love. But I find that there is a dark beauty in it. As I look across a vast expanse of bog, the grasses appear almost golden beneath the leaden silver sky; shafts of light pick through the swollen clouds without warning, lighting up the landscape for a moment like a searchlight seeking the wildlife I know must be out there.

After an hour or so the last hillock gives way to my first view of the sea. A smear of bright sands breaks the blue of the water from the green of the fertile land just back from the coast, and my pace quickens as I realise I am nearly there. The final obstacle is a dense thicket of sand dunes, as high as cliffs and as soft as butter. Lines of footprints weave their way between them but I have something else in mind – when confronted with a sand dune, the only way for me is to take a deep breath, launch my first foot over the edge and run down shrieking with a grin on my face, my heels digging great holes into the sands as I fly.

There is no more exhilarating way to arrive on a beach and I find I am giggling to myself as I take in the view. I have lucked out – not another soul can be seen. At least not a human one; there are plenty of gannets diving for fish offshore. Google Sandwood Bay and estimates of its length that range anywhere from one mile to two will come up. Suffice to say this is a whole lot of sand.

And it is beautiful. The Atlantic waves have smoothed the sands here as flat as the top of a fresh jar of Ovaltine. Those dunes at the beach's back stand proudly sprouting apple-green grass in defiance of the wind, the rain and the idiots like myself who appear from nowhere to run down them daily. On either side of this sculpted, sandy haven are bulky, dark cliffs, the folds between them picked out in milky sunlight. And in the middle of it all, a woman in a bright green jacket that was once her mum's sits on an island of rock.

The weather closed in somewhat after my walk and so I arrived at the Kylesku Hotel dripping from my waterproofs and scraping bedraggled sausages of wet hair from my face. The woman on reception looked up at me as if this was exactly who she expected to see standing in front of her, and in precisely this condition. Nobody is expected to look chic and put together on a blustery day in the Highlands, after all. And thank goodness for that.

"I assume you want to eat with us tonight?" she asks me as I fill in the check-in form. She can be presumptuous here; there is quite literally nowhere else to eat that isn't someone's house for miles around. And anyway, this hotel is meant to have some truly excellent seafood. We agree on a table for 7pm.

I am not disappointed when the staff settle me into a booth between the dining room and the bar area, bring me a gin and tonic, and hand me a menu. My eyes focus in on Ullapool oysters, hand-dived scallops and whole cracked brown crab, but it is the blackboard of specials that really grabs my attention. Langoustines, it tells me, are not available because Hamish, the fisherman who lands his catch daily at the jetty just outside, will not harvest them when they are berrying (carrying eggs). This is to keep fishing sustainable and gets my backing. Besides, there is also lobster.

I could also have had mussels from Loch Glendhu, just outside my bedroom window and the home of the highest waterfall in Britain. I have spread an Ordnance Survey map out on the table and almost instantly find myself engaged in conversation with the man tending the bar. I tell him I am thinking of walking to the waterfall but have heard it's a tough slog. "Ooh, I wouldnae bother," he offers. "There's not really a path and it's all bog. You only get to the top anyway, so you can't really see it."

Further chat about sturdy hiking boots, tough terrain and lack of time ensues, and we determine that he should book me on the boat trip on the loch instead. Since this will mean a twelve-noon start the next day I order another whisky, and am last to leave the bar that night.

The boat trip at Kylesku is run by David and James, and leaves from the jetty just outside the hotel. This is where the ferry used to run across to Kylestrome, a short journey by water that saved some one hundred miles by land. The great sweep of concrete that is the Kylesku Bridge changed all that in 1984 and the first thing James points out after leaving the jetty is the old ferry, which shut up shop that same year and was hauled ashore to be abandoned to the elements. Flowers now grow through its gently rotting deck.

A bit further up the loch we pass the mussel farm. "They're babies at this time of year," says James; "you can't see them without a microscope. You put a rope in the water and they stick, then they're stripped off after a year and put onto a net. The more fibres, the more you'll fit, tonnes of them. Then they're harvested at three years old."

Shortbread is passed around and we head onwards to the waterfall. As we approach David shouts excitedly from the wheelhouse: "Golden eagle!" We all look up towards the Stack of Glencoul, a tortoise-head-shaped lump of rock that presides over the loch, and watch this dark speck wheel beneath the clouds in search of prey.

There is plenty of wildlife out here. James tells me that the Reay Forest Estate, which surrounds us, is home to some 3,500 deer. "They have to cull about five hundred a year; people pay to come and hunt." This is the 'other' Highlands, I realise; that of the wealthy hunting, shooting and fishing brigade who fly into the vast estates they and their friends own. This one is owned by the Duke of Westminster, who also owns most of Mayfair in London. The current duke, Hugh Grosvenor, is not yet thirty and is one of the richest people in Britain. It's a trust that really owns the land – of which there is some hundred thousand acres – so it's not like Hugh could just sell it, but it is still staggering that one person can control such a hefty, and important, chunk of Scotland.

Nature rumbles on though, of course, and at the far end of the loch Eas a' Chual Aluinn is doing just that. The highest waterfall in Britain has a drop of some two hundred metres (Niagara Falls is more like fifty) and flows year-round. "It's fed by a loch, but the rain makes it better," says James as we all stare wistfully at this raging torrent of water, a couple of hundred metres off and partially hidden behind a sloping cliff. This is, of course, far taller than the waterfall at Smoo Cave, but I can't help thinking that proximity is rather important when it comes to watching falling water. I am impressed, but cannot feel it in my bones.

James had also explained that geologists get very excited about this area, and back on dry land I was keen to see the reason why. This is something called the Moine Thrust, and although there is rather a lot of detail we could go into about its geology, the gist of it is this: this is where America bashed into Britain.

The rocks here were once – and we're talking sixty million years ago here – joined to North America, and today these older rocks that sailed in from the west sit on top of the younger rocks they collided with. Seeing old rock on top of young is extremely rare, and this is what gets those geologists so excited.

The Moine Thrust runs for about one hundred miles from Durness across the north-westernmost corner of mainland Scotland to the Isle of Skye. Knockan Crag, about twenty miles south of Kylesku, is the best place to see it. Here the thrust is more than six miles wide, and there's a handy visitor centre that explains the geology.

I park in the small car park and walk up the hundred metres or so to a shelter that is in fact a series of information panels. Here I discover that two geologists called Peach and Horne should really be as famous as Darwin. They studied the rocks here and laid the foundations for modern plate tectonic theory. The British Geological Survey still makes use of their observations today, and I for one learn something here that will stay with me forever – that the plates are still moving at about the speed my fingernails grow.

Although my dad studied geology and would have happily spent hours poking about here, geology just isn't really my thing (sorry, Dad), and besides, it has started to rain. I peer up through the raindrops at the rock face above me and down at the path slowly turning to puddle beneath my feet. I decide to retreat to the car.

This part of Scotland has long been considered remote, and its distance from the urban centres of Scotland and the bulk of the country's population put it far down the list when it came to investment in roads. But then, the EU. The EU allocates funds to its poorest regions to help with economic development, and the Highlands have been receiving some of the highest payments per person in the UK. Some of this has been spent on roads, those vital links between communities, and the very drivers of the tourism that is now pouring in and bringing cash with it.

On many of the roads I have travelled in recent days I have seen large signs. They are white and deep blue, the flag of the EU standing beside the words: *Project Part Financed by the European Union: Europe and Scotland Making it Work Together*. I have seen similar signs in Wales but can't recall a single one I have seen in England. This cannot be because England doesn't receive similar funding (Cornwall and the Tees Valley most certainly do), and I wonder whether Scotland's vote to remain in the EU in the 2016 referendum was helped along by these signs. When people can see what they are actually getting out of something they are far more likely to support it, after all. I wonder if England would have voted differently had similar signs been more visible there. I fear for the state of these roads, and the Highlands more generally, once the UK stands outside the EU.

The standard of remote Highland hotels, though, is quite astonishingly good. And fresh from my very pleasant stay at the Kylesku Hotel, I found myself checking in at the classy bar area of the Summer Isles Hotel in Achiltibuie.

Achiltibuie's location can best be summed up as really far from everywhere else. It's a long way along a single-track road from the main north-south highway, and when you get here it's rather hard to put your finger on exactly where 'here' is. The Summer Isles Hotel feels like somewhere of importance, pulling in well-to-do visitors – largely, it would seem, couples from England – but everything in the village is strung out along the lochside road and there is no cluster of buildings that could be described as a village centre.

But there is a marvellous restaurant, one that I had booked a table at many weeks in advance. Salt Seafood Kitchen is tiny and I knew that, despite being open only a year or so, it was extremely popular.

I see why immediately. I have some of the best scallops I have ever had that night, overlooking an inky loch dotted with islands (those Summer Isles). I also get my fingers coated in the juices of some truly exceptional langoustines, and push my stomach to its maximum capacity with a delicious lobster mac and cheese.

When I start expounding to the waitress about how wonderful it all is, Suzie the owner comes out of the kitchen and blushingly accepts the compliments tumbling out of my mouth. "I spent some time in Glasgow and London," she tells me, "but I wanted to come back home, and wanted something to make it possible."

The restaurant has certainly done that, and if the Highlands has even a few dozen more Suzies – and I'm certain that it does – then perhaps we are on the cusp of a renaissance here. Or at the very least, the opening of a whole host of fabulous new places to eat lobster.

CHAPTER NINE

Out to the Isles

As I travelled around the farthest reaches of the Highlands I found that I was starting to dislike other English people. Perhaps it was the grumpiness that can set in on any long, tiring trip but it was feeling an awful lot like I spent much of my time listening to retired English couples moaning that they couldn't get in anywhere they would like to.

One especially disgruntled couple came and sat with me the morning I was holed up at the Summer Isles Hotel waiting for the rain to pass. "We always used to get special offers at Torridon," the wife remarked as she sipped a cappuccino and her husband snapped open the *Telegraph* with a flourish. "Now they haven't done one for over a year and they couldn't take us this weekend. That's why we're here." She said the word 'here' with a sort of dismayed sigh, a head shake and an appraising look around the lounge. Its cosy sofas facing the sea and its chirpy staff busying away at the coffee machine clearly weren't to her liking.

"It's all down to this bloody North-West 500," the husband chimed in over his glasses, getting its name wrong and glaring at me. "There didn't used to be anyone up here; now we can't get in anywhere."

At this point I began to explain that in fact it was rather good for local businesses that there were slightly more than a handful of people travelling through the area these days. The wife fixed me with a wrinkly stare and screeched, in that contemptuous voice seemingly solely reserved for the elderly entitled, "And we should care?!"

Weary and more than ready to leave them to their indignation, my parting shot was that, yes, in fact they should care. Not least because if businesses can't attract enough people they tend to close down, but also because the Highlands are not a museum and that people do actually need to make a living. I swept out of the room, hearing the *Telegraph* snap back as I left.

Fortunately I was off to the Outer Hebrides, the part of the United Kingdom that is said to be the happiest.[30] Hopefully I would meet some more positive people there.

The ferry to Stornoway, the largest town in the Outer Hebrides, leaves from Ullapool. I was booked on the next day's evening service – and I was worried. The weather had been wet and windy for several days and my planned boat trip to the Summer Isles had been cancelled twice in a row. The most visited app on my phone was fast becoming the CalMac Ferries app, with its sailing updates displayed with red warning triangles.

Nothing seemed to be cancelled, though, and on my arrival in Ullapool the town was its usual bustling self, the harbourfront line-up of wee whitewashed buildings winking back any shaft of sunlight that passed through the clouds.

I have always loved Ullapool and today it seems even more enticing, bathed in sunshine and the promise of an adventure to the Outer Hebrides. Excited to have reached the jumping-off point for the Isles at last, I pop into the West Coast Delicatessen, buzzing with a desire to stock up on local produce for the picnics and self-catering nights in to come.

Naturally I buy far too much. Locally smoked cheese, some blue cheese from Tain on the east coast, a great slab of venison salami and a bagload of homemade shortbread. The guy on the counter certainly knows a loss leader when he sees one and continues feeding me samples as we talk. My mantra becomes: "Ooh yes, just a couple of hundred grams of that one as well, please." I leave with two full bags.

There is something about Ullapool that puts me in a shopping mood – something about it being the last point on the mainland before the wilder Outer Hebrides, perhaps – and so I continued to the Ullapool Bookshop. I had become fascinated by the local interest sections of independent bookstores. Every time I passed one I felt myself drawn inexorably in to peruse shelves of slender paperbacks focused on very specific local history stories, and hardback coffee-table tomes of gorgeous Scottish wildlife or landscape photography. I pick up a guidebook to the Outer Hebrides and retreat back to my hotel before I spend any more money.

I'd be surprised if there's a Scot in the Isles who doesn't owe something to CalMac. Because it is truly a fantastic company. Now I'm not normally one to fall in love with large companies, but CalMac deserves some devotion. For a start it seems to be run by human beings. Ones who actually care about getting you to where you want to be, and who might even help you get there.

I had had to change one ferry ticket in advance of my trip. I had booked the wrong date and it was entirely my own stupid fault. But when I called the (free) phone number a helpful man simply changed my booking for me. Just changed it. He didn't ask me for my cat's maiden name or a booking reference longer than my credit-card number and not appearing on any confirmation ever sent. He didn't suck his teeth and threaten admin fees or a cancellation fee. He didn't even put me on hold to speak to some mythical supervisor. He simply changed the date and time of my booking and emailed me a fresh confirmation before I was even off the phone. Frankly, I was flabbergasted.

What is more important is of course actually getting people from A to B. And even on this wild and windy day, CalMac were doing just that; reliably departing pretty much on schedule around the Western Isles and ploughing out to sea in their stable yet sleek black-and-white ferries.

This is a lifeline of a service. That cancelled Summer Isles boat trip wasn't vital to anyone but CalMac are responsible for getting kids to school and nurses to work. And so I doubt there is anyone in the Isles who doesn't owe CalMac gratitude for something, from the chance to get to a distant but important funeral on short notice, to the simple delight of being able to get home to the family in time for dinner.

On my ferry crossing CalMac are bringing the local shinty team home from the mainland. At least I presume they are heading home after a match rather than preparing for one, given the amount of drained, squashed beer cans sitting on the table in the bar. That bar is the heart of a CalMac crossing, and I sit eating CalMac and cheese (see what they've done there?) and fish pie as the sun dips towards the Minch and the bundled shinty sticks clatter in rhythm with the boat.

My favourite place on board a ferry is always the outer deck, and so I spend the first half-hour or so after sailaway standing atop the MV *Loch Seaforth*. The sail-out from Ullapool is spectacular and the weather has come good, flaring up into the sort of sunset only western Scotland can do. The waters of Loch Broom are almost flat calm, the ripples only as deep as softly dimpled glass. On the horizon sits the dark hulk of land, a black sash between the deep blue of the water and the mandarin orange of the sky. A man standing next to me points out the triangular fin of a porpoise some twenty metres from the boat, and I finally get to see the Summer Isles, scattered across the water on the starboard side. If my time in the Outer Hebrides is to be made up of moments like these, I can see why the Isles are the happiest place in the UK.

The most surprising thing about Stornoway is not that there is a lively community living a very nice life out here in the Isles, but that it is still a deeply religious place. This is highly unusual for the UK today and it was fortunate that the woman on reception when I checked into my hotel asked me if I had enough petrol. It was Saturday night, you see, and nothing would be open tomorrow. Not even Tesco. This is something that simply would not have occurred to me. The following morning Stornoway is stone-cold silent. As I make my way out through the town there is barely a car on the roads, and sure enough Tesco sits shut up and unable to sell me food or petrol.

One thing that is open on a Sunday is Dun Carloway, though this might have something to do with the fact that it would be impossible to close. This is a broch, a type of prehistoric tower in circular stone that is unique to Scotland. The word 'dun' comes from the Gaelic for hill or hill fort, and the broch stands on a naturally high rocky outcrop above Loch Roag.

The story behind life in these structures is a mysterious one. Although Dun Carloway is one of Scotland's best-preserved brochs, there is so much that is unknown here. Even Historic Environment Scotland can only say that it "was probably constructed about 200 BC", and that it is "said to have been used as a stronghold by members of the Morrison Clan during the 1500s".

What can definitely be said is that this is an exhilarating spot to visit. At nine metres tall the broch stands close to its presumed original height, and it is possible to clamber over much of it, striding along the top of drystone walls now sprouting grass and ducking through ancient doorways to walk with stooped back between the broch's double skin of thick walls.

Even more mesmerising is another ancient site just a few miles away: the Standing Stones of Calanais. Growing up in Wiltshire, school trips were more often than not to Avebury, a stone circle that is part of the same UNESCO World Heritage Site as Stonehenge. I remember my mum chaperoning a trip to this ancient stone circle when I was about seven or eight and still wore a thin, light green checked dress to school in the summer. I remember sitting on the grass, the morning dew soaking into the fabric, as I drew pictures of the stones and took rubbings of them with a dark HB pencil.

Avebury remains one of my favourite places to this day. But what Calanais has that Avebury simply doesn't is an elemental location. The stones here stand atop a ridge on the very edge of land. Here on the far western coast of Scotland the sky is ever massive. It stretches unyieldingly in every direction, uninterrupted by either mountain or building until it peters out in a milky line atop the landscape. It makes the Calanais stones feel like they must be the tallest thing for miles around, the one in the centre an imposing 4.8 metres in height.

I stand in awe for several minutes, trying to take photographs that will capture the atmosphere at this five-thousand-year-old site. This proves impossible and so I just wander instead, stepping right up to the stones to lay my palms on them and feel the heat they have taken from the sun. They are an integral part of the landscape, as connected to the peaty ground as any naturally lying stone I might have clambered over on a walk. I could never prefer them to Avebury's but they do run a very close second.

My main plan for the day was to get to Uig. This is not something to be taken lightly. The west coast of Scotland is heavily indented, its bulky outline broken up by inlets and lochs that constantly push the road inland in search of a dry route from A to B. It may only have been ten miles as the crow flies from Calanais to my B&B at Uig Sands but by road this is a journey of more than twenty, completing almost three sides of a square to get there.

It is a long pootle out to Uig and so I wasn't all that happy to discover that, being Sunday, my B&B was not offering dinner.

Naturally the village shop was closed too and I was hungry for more than the cheese and venison cuts I had picked up in Ullapool. For dinner I would have to head out immediately to catch the local café's Sunday opening hours. I wasn't thrilled at the prospect of more driving.

The nearest café was out at Gallan Head, about three miles further from the main road than Uig Sands. This is a remote spot and I am not surprised to learn that it is ex-MoD land. For some sixty years locals were unable to enjoy the expansive views from this high promontory that claims to be Britain's north-westernmost point because the military had the entire site closed off. Today it is owned by a community trust, and on my visit to this special spot I found Fiona cooking up chowder entirely from scratch at The Edge Café.

This is not Fiona's home but it certainly feels like it is. I sit at a large blue table in the dining room as Fiona busies away in the adjoining kitchen, chopping up vegetables and boiling water. She brings me tea and keeps popping out for a chat. I learn that she moved here with her ex-husband because it was a place she knew her mother-in-law would not follow them to. "She would have followed us to France, but not here," she tells me.

"People say it's the middle of nowhere," Fiona adds wistfully as I stare out of the window at nothing but sea and sky. "But it has its own centre."

All of that evening it rains, and overnight I listen to the thrum of raindrops on the roof above me. I had resolved that a two-night stay means I needn't get up too early but the next morning I go downstairs to make a cup of tea and discover that it is wall-to-wall blue sky. I fear that this break between weathers will disappear as quickly as it has arrived and so I abandon the idea of showering, quickly down a steaming bowl of porridge and head out the back of the house to find the very best view I have seen in all my life.

From where my feet stand sinking into lush green grass, the

land undulates down to meet water so clear it's impossible to tell how deep it might be. Just beyond this ribbon of resting seawater a curve of creamy sands divides one patch of water from the next. In this the mountains stand reflected, a mirror image of the ridge of brooding Lewisian gneiss that forms the horizon and splits this paradise into earth and sky.

This is Uig Sands. Or rather, it is part of it. I romp down across the grass and onto a small headland slightly further out towards the sea. I turn to look to my left and suddenly there is more – a vast expanse of sculpted flat sands left between one set of hills and the next by the retreating Atlantic. I stand beaming to myself, unable to believe that I have got so lucky as to see this place on a day as sun-soaked as this. "You've won the lottery," Richard the B&B owner shouts over to me from the main house.

I am keen to leave the day's first footprints in the sands and so I begin the short scramble down the dunes to reach the main beach, and several miles of perfect powder. On either side of the beach salmon rivers flow into the sea, a few rocky cliffs mark the boundary between dry land and sodden sand, and still the sky is cloudless and dazzling blue.

My inner child has been released and I run across the beach, whooping and jumping into any patches that look especially soft. The sand has been formed into a never-ending ripple, the ridges of which disappear underfoot with one heavy footstep, slushing downwards into the watery sands around them. I find myself mesmerised by what happens when I put my weight on this moulded sandscape, the shape of it slipping around my foot as if I have any control whatsoever over nature.

I walk for a couple of hours, weaving across the sands. On the far side of the beach I know that there is a distillery and so I aim for the river it sits on and find myself scrambling once again, this time to get back up to the road.

The Red River Distillery (or Abhainn Dearg) gets its name from the river, which in turn gets its name from the time when the local distillers attacked the taxmen on the bridge where they were supposed to pay their dues. It is said that they spilled enough blood to stain the river red. "I don't know if it's true or not," the woman I find manning the shed-like tasting room at the distillery says, "but it's a good story."

This is the first (legal) distillery on Lewis for almost two hundred years, ever since the one in Stornoway was torn down after the owner 'got religion'. The buildings were once a fish farm, and today there isn't a lot to see. There is, however, a young single malt you can taste, and if you're visiting after 2018 there should even be a ten-year-old whisky.

It's also just generally a great place for a blether. I sit on a stool at the bar, shedding jumpers in the unexpected warmth of the Hebridean sunshine, and hear about Uig. "The primary school here has about fifteen kids now," says my whisky-purveying new best friend. "There were thirty or forty when I was there, but the population has gone down. People pass away or go away. I'm twenty and there's nobody here my age now; they've all left for uni."

This is the curse of the Isles, but on a day like this it's hard to see why you'd want to leave for anywhere else. The trouble, perhaps, is the quiet. Tourism is the great regenerator, bringing people who are happy to pay for a place to stay and something to eat. But at the moment the Outer Hebrides could be said to have the most to lose from the new North Coast 500 route. So many people have been captivated by the desire to tick off a bucket-list road trip but perhaps some of them would otherwise have chosen the Isles for their travels in Scotland. It is just so quiet here in comparison. Perhaps the grumpy couple from the Summer Isles Hotel should make their next holiday here. Though I'm not sure that I would wish them on anyone.

Uig is best known for the chessmen that were found here in around 1831, allegedly by a cow that was rooting around with its horns in a sandbank. Fortunately, the cow's human companion spotted that this was something rather magnificent and soon ninety-three pieces of ivory carved in the twelfth century were reclaimed from the sands.

Although today most of these live in the British Museum in London (and some in the National Museum of Scotland in Edinburgh), six are now to be found at the new Museum nan Eilean at Lews Castle in Stornoway. Since the road southwards to Harris – where I am headed – can only be picked up just south of Stornoway, I decide to pop back to the big smoke for a quick blast of Wi-Fi and a poke around the museum.

I find a small but utterly contemporary space, all glass-box displays and video screens. In the centre stand the chessmen – and they are really quite astonishingly ornate. They are some eight hundred years old but they look as if they could have been carved last week. One in particular charms me; his facial expression one of sighing boredom, his head resting on a weary palm. He reminds me of a bored spouse watching their partner try on the umpteenth grey jumper in a high-street changing room.

I also learn that the cow-rifling story might not be quite the truth. At Uig a sign had told me, clear as day, that the chessmen were found in 1831 by Malcolm Macleod. Here, though, the signage says different; that the chessmen were found in a sand dune in Uig, either in Mealista or Ardroil, probably hidden in a small chamber, and that: *There are many local stories but it's a mystery who found the chessmen and exactly when.* Like the story of the red river, it may not be true but it is a good story.

I couldn't linger long at the museum because I had an appointment with a mountain. I was keen to climb An Clisham, the highest point in the Outer Hebrides.

An Clisham is on Harris, Lewis's semi-detached next-door neighbour. Despite the different identities of these two island communities, Lewis and Harris are not in fact separate islands. The two are joined by six miles of moorland, the border between them running across from Loch Reasort in the west to Loch Seaforth in the east. Despite following along on my satnav and craning my head out of the window on the drive southwards, from the A859 the border isn't obvious at all.

Neither is An Clisham. Despite its status as the tallest point, this is not an especially popular mountain to climb – at least not by mainland Scottish standards. This is partly because it is not a Munro. It is about two hundred metres too short to be classed as one, but that is not to say it's an easy climb.

It's one that doesn't follow an obvious path, for a start. Even on exiting the car in the car park the path through the sodden, boggy landscape isn't exactly leaping out at me. And as I look up towards the summit, even though I am standing in bright sunshine, the top is obscured by heavy clouds.

Nobody wants to start climbing a mountain with wet feet and so I layer up with every waterproof item I have and set off with great concentration, picking the driest-looking route along the river. The path becomes more obvious as I get used to picking out the browner bits of this mucky green landscape with my feet – these tend to be more solid, more mud and less water.

The walk becomes a trudge as the path scuds to a halt and the flank of An Clisham rears up steeply ahead of me. Now it is all about stepping from rock to rock and avoiding sinking my feet into the springy grass gaps between the boulders. A few burns run down the mountainside and I am careful to avoid them. Although at first they seem to offer an obvious rock path, they often end up at steep-sided drop-offs that only water   and definitely not humans – can chart a course over.

It's a tough walk and I'm too exhausted from the effort to think of much more than putting one foot inexorably in front of the other. But I can see a bright red Gore-Tex jacket far above me, moving with purpose up the mountain, and I have already been overtaken by a sprightly man who is practically running up. I am not alone.

This is a relief as I reach the plateau at the top. My phone tells me that I am at 750 metres above sea level – the summit is 799 so can surely not be much further. Even better, that red Gore-Tex jacket has materialised as a person in front of me. I imagine that the seventy-odd-year-old man happily picking his way down must already be on the return from the summit, and ask him how much further it is.

"I haven't been to the top," he says. "I've been up before and thought we'd get a view today but there's no point in this weather." The weather has indeed closed in but there are breaks in the clouds and I have my compass at the ready. And anyway, for me part of the point is to stand atop the highest point in the Outer Hebrides – as well as to prove that I can conquer what is not easily conquered. The climb is slightly easier now, too: more a scramble up sturdy rocks than a suck-it-and-see stagger up a hillside.

So I follow the compass onwards and upwards, peering up every so often to see if those clouds will part even just for a second. Suddenly a wall that looks man-made leers out of the mists and I remember that there's a wall built around the trig point here. This is the summit, and when I clamber over the wall I find it is entirely sheltered from the wind – and already occupied by the walker who overtook me. He is determined to wait for the weather to clear; I am just happy to eat my sandwich. We hunker down and refuel, discussing the other hills we have climbed and agreeing that An Clisham is tougher than some Munros. It is certainly tougher than Schiehallion.

I have quickly had enough of being in the slightly damp air of the clouds and so I say my goodbyes and begin to pick my way back down to the plateau – and finally see the view. I don't quite see it all in one piece, but what I do see is incredible. I am surrounded by towering peaks, a series of sculpted mounds that encircle a flat, boggy landscape that runs down to a sea loch. An Clisham stands tall at my back, now suddenly visible for a few seconds – just long enough to grab a selfie – and then seemingly drawing the curtains around herself once more and disappearing behind the clouds. It has all been worth it. And even on my return to the car, my feet are still not wet.

I have two nights on Harris and grand plans for my one full day here. My base is at Borvemor Cottages, a series of cottages and steadings that sits on the west coast close to Luskentyre Bay. This is surely Scotland's most famous beach, a striking swirl of white sands and turquoise waters that is reminiscent of Australia's more famous Whitehaven Beach. Luskentyre is of course best seen at low tide, when the sands are free of the sea and you can walk out across the inlet, crunching tiny purple-and-white shells underfoot as you go. Despite being shattered from my hike, I decide that I must go to Luskentyre now, because it is low tide and the sun is out. This may not happen again tomorrow, or indeed for some time.

My feet are aching but soon I do not notice. Luskentyre is easy enough to walk out onto, crossing a small series of dunes from the car park, and had I not just been at Uig Sands I'm sure I would have declared this to be the most beautiful thing I had ever seen instead. With the sun out, it is easily living up to its moniker of 'the Scottish Caribbean', and there's even a rainbow arching above it all.

I end up walking for ages, feeling the sun on my face and forgetting all about my protesting leg muscles. A few degrees warmer and this would be the perfect beach holiday destination. I wonder if perhaps Scotland has in fact been saved by its weather. Otherwise 1970s package tourism may well have landed here and built its high-rise hotels right across this glorious landscape. Those rainy days aren't all bad, I decide.

The next day I'm heading to the south coast and am keen to pick up a takeaway from a place that is the stuff of local legend. Croft 36 is no more than a jaunty blue-and-white shed marked by the purple sign of the Eat Drink Hebrides food trail. This is a sign I keep on seeing – for everything from smokehouses to hand-dived scallops – and one that I grow to love, a mark of excellence in local produce that can be followed throughout the Outer Hebrides. There is no need to eat poorly here.

At Croft 36 there are no staff. This is an honesty box made large: a shack full of pies, pastries and soups homemade by a woman called Julie and left out for lunches or to take back home for later. I munch on a tasty venison pie and grab some home-baked bread for the next day's breakfast before setting off to drive Harris's most famous scenic drive.

This is called the Golden Road. It loops along the east coast of the island, a coastline sometimes referred to as 'the Bays' for its endless line-up of mini fjords. Locals will argue over whether the 'golden' nickname comes from the vital importance of this road to the hamlets that lie along it or the expense invested to build it, but either way it's a beautiful drive.

I begin winding my way northwards on a single-track road that hardly seems to need its passing places, so few other cars are out and about. The scenery is wild, the cold grey gneiss rock barely allowing the grass to break through, the road a narrow strip of tarmac clinging improbably to the ripples of hardy land that rise up from the sea but somehow remain flooded by it. The water encroaches from all sides, threatening to join Atlantic to loch with just one wave.

My destination is the Harris Tweed Exhibition at Drinishader. Here I find a large white former schoolhouse fashioned into an engaging museum that tells the story of Harris tweed, or *Clò Mòr*, the Gaelic for 'big cloth'. Harris is not the only island to be allowed to make authentic Harris tweed – it can also be made on Lewis, in the Uists or on Barra – but it must always be handwoven in the weavers' own homes. There is no Harris tweed factory, only the Harris Tweed Authority, the guardians of the cloth, its quality and its reputation.

Today they seem to be doing rather well. Harris tweed has been used by Norton & Sons Savile Row tailors, London-based luxury accessories brand Radley, and big-name fashion designers Hugo Boss and Ralph Lauren. Alfa Romeo even used Harris tweed to upholster the seats of their MiTo car.

For years, though, the industry was in decline. It was said that the Outer Hebrides' greatest export was people, and the dwindling population was mirrored in the decline in the number of weavers. But then in 2004 Donald John Mackay received a phone call from America – it was Nike asking for nine thousand metres of his tweed to use in their shoes. His shed, beside his home in Luskentyre, was rather busy that summer and the tweed's reputation soared.

Back at Borvemor I discover that my host, Scott, is in fact hiding his very own loom in his shed. "We used to have a weaver here," he tells me, "but he lived two miles away. You have to live and weave on your own croft and the Harris Tweed Association told me, 'You'll never call that Harris tweed.'" A look of defiance crosses his face, and his hands find their way onto his hips. "So I'm learning. This *will* be Harris tweed one day."

A stack of rolled tweed on the cabinet behind the loom catches my eye and I ask after it. Scott pulls out a roll, telling me that it's the herringbone he used to make his wedding anniversary suit. His wife Margaret beams with pride behind him as he talks gently about the things they have made and produced here on their croft. "Margaret built a drystone-wall black house," he tells me as Margaret's proud expression fades immediately into humble. "There on the wall is her certificate from the Dry Stone Walling Association." Only in the Outer Hebrides would you find such a gung-ho couple, I think. Oh, and by the way, these two are seventy if they're a day.

My final night on Harris was spent at Talla na Mara, its wooden walls so new they still gleam with unweathered brightness. The West Harris community own and operate this as an arts and entertainment centre. It has a restaurant with views out over the sea in two directions, and behind it sits a row of houses, built as affordable homes for local families.

It is wonderful. I am welcomed like an old friend, with chat about the weather and what I've been up to today, and seated at a table really meant for four so that I can enjoy the view from a better vantage point. I order fish and chips and wonder whether I could in fact live here. I have been charmed by the warmth of the Isles and begin to understand what Fiona meant about the Isles having their own centre.

Suddenly there is a hubbub behind me. The sun has started to set, the clouds above it taking on a deep magenta hue unlike any I have seen before. I leap up from my seat and walk out onto the terrace with pretty much everyone else in the restaurant.

In one direction the sun is lighting up the landscape like a floodlight; in the other the great orb is sinking into the Sound of Taransay. Over the next few minutes a pink as sugary-sweet as candyfloss spreads across the sky. The lightest clouds take on the lightest colour, the thicker ones remaining purple to create a marbled sunset that everybody is trying to capture.

I snap away with my iPhone, trying to snare on screen the very best sunset I have ever seen. Gradually pink sinks into purple and the contrast between the bright patches of sky lit by the descending sun and the brooding darkness of the storm clouds gathering above the landscape gets ever more intense. One side of the sky appears bruised, mottled indigo and violet by the violent clouds, while the other is lit in delicate lemon-gold so perfect I find myself imagining it as a halo atop an angel's head.

It is awesome – in the very truest sense of the word. Even by the Hebrides' high standards this is an epic sunset, and we look at each other, all of us, with wonder and excitement. "Just another day in the Outer Hebrides," one man says with a contented sigh. Yep, I can see why these might be the UK's happiest people.

CHAPTER TEN

The Uists and Barra

Before I left Borvemor, Scott insisted that I must walk down to the local beach. I was booked on a late-morning CalMac crossing to Berneray but he was adamant and, since he had been such a thoughtful host, I didn't like to disappoint him.

So off I went, down to the back gate of their property to make my way across the grassland at the back of the dunes, all the while checking the time and feeling more beholden than excited to see this beach. Surely it couldn't be better than Uig.

Well, by now I really should know to listen to Scottish people when they tell me something is worth seeing. Because what I find is a glorious stretch of sands, sculpted into huge wave-like humps. Through the sands is a strange channel, carved as if by a raging river that has long since dried up. Its sides stand about half a metre high, wrinkled like a Viennetta and tempting me to see if they can take my weight. They can't, crumpling like tissue paper beneath me, and I become absorbed in playing with the sand once again.

I am sad to be leaving Harris, but there is far more to the Outer Hebrides than just the largest island of Harris and Lewis

– in fact there are more than a hundred islands and skerries here – and this morning I am heading south, to South Uist via Berneray, North Uist, Benbecula and Grimsay.

From the Scottish mainland the Outer Hebrides appear on the horizon as one, a bit like a smudged line on a painting. They are sometimes collectively referred to as the Long Island but they are far from one homogenous land mass. I had already seen the difference between the dramatic peaty moorland of Lewis and the chunky peaks of Harris, and now I was to travel further south, to set foot on as many islands as possible over the course of not nearly enough time.

The ferry to Berneray leaves from Leverburgh. This is Harris's second-largest village and it sits overlooking the Sound of Harris, a roughly eight-mile-wide stretch of water that is one of two main passages through the Outer Hebrides for ships passing from the Atlantic Ocean to the Minch.

It is also scattered with a quite astounding number of islands, islets and reefs. This means that the ferry crossing is far from a straight steam across. The hour-long journey is in fact a winding cruise through narrow channels and between jutting rocks that proceeds at a pace sedate enough to spot seals and dolphins and discuss at length whether that bird everyone is looking at is a cormorant or a shag.

The ferry crossing is certainly part of the experience of travelling through the Outer Hebrides, but it is one that may one day become a thing of the past. Plans are afoot to build a bridge,[31] both here and over the Sound of Barra further south, preventing bottlenecks at the ferries, linking the islands and their services, and making the idea of an Outer Hebrides road trip more appealing to more people in the process.

I love the ferry crossing, though, and on this late-autumn day it is like a sailing in the Adriatic, reminiscent of cruising from one Croatian island to the next. The sun is beating down from an almost entirely clear blue sky, its light bouncing off water as flat calm as a bathtub. I sit outside on the top deck and listen to an English couple on one side exclaiming that this could be the Med; a trio of men on the other, dressed in chunky work boots and speaking Gaelic. As we push through the sound, the water ripples up like satin, and on arrival in Berneray the harbour waters appear like glass.

A more perfect beach day would be hard to imagine, and so I head immediately for West Beach. Not because I'm desperate to run down yet another sandy dune but because this particular beach was the focal point of a rather embarrassing Thai tourism campaign back in 2009 – and I want to see if it does look anything at all like Thailand.

Well, it doesn't, frankly. Yes, there are the white sands and azure seas of cliché, but offshore are the rather prominent peaks of the Harris mountains. Much was made in the media of these peaks being the giveaway that the folks in Thai tourism had decided to pull an image from the internet rather than invest in sending a photographer to Kai Bae Beach. But to me, there are so many more differences. Those sand dunes for a start, sloping upwards to meet the tufty grass. They don't look a thing like the dense thicket of palm trees that lines the back of Kai Bae Beach. And then there are the waters, the frothing Atlantic surf that could never be mistaken for the lapping Gulf of Thailand. The sands here are whiter too; at Kai Bae there is an almost dirty golden hue.

To my mind the Outer Hebrides don't look like anywhere else on earth. The landscape here is unique and I am constantly walking through a type of terrain that is found nowhere outside of the exposed west coasts of Scotland and Ireland. This is a type of low-lying grassy plain that in Gaelic is called machair. Although machair is one of the rarest types of landscape in Europe, in the Outer Hebrides it is as common as muck.

Behind the dune ridge of every beach I have visited lies a bouncy grass and wildflower carpet. Here water is pervasive, often seeping up from beneath the sandy soil, forming into small lochs or carving its way through the grass to expose the soft sand and shell beneath. That water could be from the sea, or fresh from the sky, but it asserts itself throughout these islands, and especially in North Uist I feel that the land is only clinging on to its place amid the waters.

I feel this even more so when I embark on a walk at Beinn Langais. I only have time for one walk on North Uist and this is the obvious one to do, leading up to the best-preserved Neolithic cairn in the Outer Hebrides, at Barpa Langais, and on to the island's only stone circle.

Despite it being a dry day following several days of sunshine, the ground underfoot is sodden. As I troop up the hill I look left and right to see that I am surrounded by lochans, a 360-degree brackish panorama of dark blue waters sunk into a landscape of brown bogland and stretching out to the ocean in every direction.

At the cairn itself heather has managed to cling on to the slopes and the grass beneath my feet is drier. I am at a high point, commanding a view over the landscape that hints at the lofty status of those likely buried here. Nobody really knows why Barpa Langais is here. It was probably a ceremonial focus for the community, but it has never been excavated by modern archaeologists and now the opening has collapsed, it is not possible (or safe) to go inside. The sign that tells me this uses the words 'recent collapse' but I suspect it has been here announcing this for some time, and find myself wondering what else is out there, gradually sinking further into the ground and the past.

I find myself sinking into the ground on the rest of the walk, the landscape as boggy as a field after a music festival. There is a trig point on the horizon and a series of wooden posts marking the way to it, but no path exists up here on the top of the Beinn and I am left alone to battle the elements.

It is well worth it. At the top of the hill the view is magnificent, more water than land, and I can just about see a route down through the heather and ferns to the stone circle at Pobull Fhinn. This is no landscaped visitor attraction; here the stones sit subsumed in the bracken, heads of grass and the leaves of ferns waving in front of them, the thick heather threatening to engulf the smaller stones. These are not the towering monoliths of Calanais or Avebury, but the dumpier rocks of Pobull Fhinn have their own beauty, a quieter one, perhaps. That they are sitting here largely undisturbed by human feet makes them all the more beguiling.

North Uist is said to have the best views of another group of islands, one that sits some forty-five miles off the outer coast of the Outer Hebrides, deserted but far from forgotten. St Kilda is a near-mythical place in the minds of many Scots, a small group of islands where life became so untenable for the dwindling local population that in 1930 they asked the government to evacuate them. This archipelago of ragged mountaintops and volcanic sea stacks now sits brooding in the Atlantic, tempting hardy souls to visit.

A few years ago I was tempted to take on the three-day steam out from Oban with Hebrides Cruises. Not normally one to get seasick, even I was concerned about the epic crossing I had heard about. There would be a pleasant first day's sail to Tobermory on Mull, but after that would follow two full days heading due west, crossing first the Minch to reach the Outer Hebrides and then that swathe of Atlantic to finally drop anchor in Village Bay on the main island of Hirta.

I spent those two days battling myself. I wanted to be out on deck or reading the library of books on St Kildan history, geology and wildlife; instead I sat with my feet up and my head against the wall, watching the horizon move several metres up in the air before swinging back downwards, seemingly beneath my feet, again.

Because it is so difficult to reach the islands, the community on St Kilda had to be entirely self-sufficient. Often cut off from the mainland for months at a time, it was almost a year before the people here found out that they had been praying for the wrong monarch when Queen Victoria took the throne, and when the first steamship of tourists landed here in 1838 the villagers ran to the reverend to tell him a ship was on fire in the bay.

St Kilda might have been extremely isolated, but it was also extremely well ordered. Each morning the able-bodied men would meet to decide on the work of the day, and each person, from the newborn to the elderly, was provided for by the community. Fuel was provided by the island's turf; food by its substantial bird population.

Boys were taught to scale the island's sheer, high cliffs as soon as they were old enough and grew up to be stocky and agile. Nature saw to it that they had a different bone structure: thicker ankles and wider feet than the mainland male, perfect for climbing Conachair, the island's highest point, which has the highest sea cliffs in Britain at 376 metres.

For almost nine months of every year, the St Kildans hunted birds. These isolated islands are home to the oldest and largest population of fulmars in Britain and the world's largest gannet colony, and these formed the basis of the islanders' diet. In the 1690s, Scottish writer Martin Martin (yep, really) visited St Kilda to write his *A Description of the Western Islands of Scotland*. He was told by the islanders that between two-hundred-odd people they had consumed 22,600 gannets in the past year and that this was less than normal.[32] The fact that this was sustainable gives some idea of how many birds nested on St Kilda.

In this regard, not much has changed. Our guide for the trip, Chris, told me that this is "the most important seabird colony in Europe", and on my visit I saw thousands of seabirds. As we sailed towards the islands and into Village Bay, the island's only safe anchorage, the odd gannet wheeling overhead became dozens, the air thickening with them as they swirled around the towering granite cliffs. Looking closer I saw that the zigzagging crags were hiding nesting puffins in their hundreds – some 140,000 pairs make this Britain's largest colony.

Our presence sent them into a frenzy, birds soaring en masse, a scattering starburst of wings and beaks. They flew out over the water or plunged across the emerald-green grass slopes of the island's central saddle, towards the low drystone remains of what were once the St Kildans' homes, huddled along one street just back from Village Bay.

Some one hundred people lived here in the nineteenth century but today the place is abandoned, the only visitors National Trust for Scotland volunteers, MoD contractors manning the radar station, and a scant few tourists, sailing in as conditions allow. In 1930 there were still eleven inhabited cottages on Hirta, and on the morning of the 29th August each one had a fire burning in its hearth. That day, though, their occupants left, and by the evening, for the first time in more than a thousand years, the last flame went out on St Kilda.

The evacuation came about because the islanders' lives became untenable. The harsh hand-to-mouth lifestyle had driven many young able-bodied islanders away, to the mainland and even as far afield as Australia, in search of the fabled better life. The tourist ships which continued to come after that first one in 1838 showed St Kildans what lay beyond the horizon – the comforts and trappings of modern life. By 1930 just thirty-six islanders remained, and only nine able-bodied men. It was not enough to sustain a community.

Today the homes of these last thirty-six St Kildans sit in varying stages of restoration, some housing National Trust for Scotland volunteers, one (Number 3) housing a small museum, but most sitting squat and roofless, the wind whipping through their open windows, the grass growing wild in their front rooms.

Behind the village looms the great mass of Conachair. This was our target for our one full day on Hirta, and as we started to make our way up The Gap, behind the village, the swirling mists cleared in patches to reveal first one awe-inspiring view and then another. We looked back to see sweeping jade-green grasslands, shaped as if they were the remains of a scooped-out ice-cream tub, and the waters of the bay winking back at us in the sunshine. Then suddenly the clouds descended, rolling down the slopes in a great, grey cloak, obscuring everything as they have always done. The weather on St Kilda can never be predicted.

The St Kildans built small stone shelters (called *cleits*) to store birds they had caught for later, and these dotted the landscape as we headed further up into the mist, always just a few metres from the sheer granite cliffs. The climb was tough, almost a trudge, and the hillside seemed to form a staircase as we thrust first one foot and then the other into its grassy side. Looking up, there was nothing to see but cloud; looking down, all was grass.

But then the clouds cleared. Suddenly the hillside flattened out and I looked up to see its crest, marked by a cairn. I also saw my first great skua, sitting in the grass just a few metres away. It was watching me with barely concealed contempt.

I had heard much about these aggressive birds, known colloquially as 'bonxies' for their habit of 'bonking' people on the head to encourage them to leave their territory, but it was not until we began our descent across the island's saddle that I started to believe the hype. Bird after swooping bird circled us, moving closer each time until they were dive-bombing our group. We huddled closer, thrusting umbrellas handle-up into the air to discourage them, but the onslaught did not stop until we staggered into the radar station at the saddle's other side, relieved to be in the shadow of its tall mast.

This mast is part of the MoD's tracking facility for their missile-testing range back over on South Uist,[33] and represents the reason why these remote islands are once again inhabited – this is the largest area in the UK for the live-firing of rockets and missiles. And this says it all. The MoD can test rockets here because there is nothing here. Nothing, that is, except epic scenery and Europe's best birdwatching. It is a truly special place.

On this trip a visit is not possible. It is too late in the year and there is too little time. There is, however, a St Kilda viewpoint marked on my map and I am keen to see whether my scepticism about being able to see St Kilda from here is justified.

The drive takes me far off my route south, forcing me around the western loop of North Uist's main road, and I am gently grumbling to myself that this is probably a waste of time. But then, with a glance to my left somewhere just past Bayhead, I think I see something. A lump on the horizon. *Surely not*, I think, but my pulse quickens. I really am keen to see St Kilda again.

The road to the viewpoint is also the road to an MoD facility of some kind, but I assume I will get nowhere near it. The viewpoint is only marked as being on this hill and I imagine it must be an open area at the summit, a blustery point where I can stand for a while and gaze out to sea. So I ignore the tiny signpost I can barely read on the right-hand side of the road and continue on my way upwards.

As I round the final corner I see immediately that this was a mistake. A tall fence rears up a few metres ahead, two men behind it suddenly alert. They look at me with serious interest as I pull up short and try to quickly execute a three-point turn while looking as innocuous as possible. Although I know I am doing nothing wrong, there is something about a checkpoint manned by uniformed people who are almost certainly armed that gets me all in a fluster and I take an eternity to turn the car around. I would be no use whatsoever as a getaway driver, it turns out.

The St Kilda viewpoint was, of course, the stopping point I had vaguely noted on my drive up, and on my second attempt I pull in at the right spot. A small square of stones has been built to contain a telescope and a carved map of the landscape. On it are marked the islands of St Kilda, and on the horizon, as clear as day, are the land masses themselves. I am blown away. To have been so privileged as to spend a whole sunny day on Hirta previously, and now to be so lucky as to see her again, drenched in sunshine and from forty-five miles distant, feels unbelievable. I can almost imagine that those fires are still burning, somehow.

St Kilda is only one example of a Scottish island community that has vanished within the last century or so. Other islands that now lack the permanent population they once had include Mingulay and Berneray to the south of Barra, and Taransay – famously the location of the BBC's *Castaway* series – off Harris.

Isolation – from services and from other, larger communities – is often the root cause, and one solution to this has been the building of causeways, linking up the islands and making travel from one to another both quicker and simpler. No ferry, after all, means no ticket to buy and no timetable to follow. Impromptu journeys are easier; the allure of island life is stronger.

But the causeways are contentious; the South Ford Causeway between Benbecula and South Uist particularly. This was built in 1982, and in 2005 played a part in the deaths of five members of the same family on the night of a terrible storm. Their cars were washed into the sea, some say because the causeway blocked the natural channel of the storm surge, causing it to be higher than it would otherwise have been and to sweep their cars off the road.

It is possible that a bridge would be better here, and might have saved those five tragically lost lives, but as ever, money is the issue. Funding from the Scottish government has allegedly been denied on cost-benefit grounds.[34]

On a calm-weather day it is hard to believe the Atlantic can be so vicious. Today as I make my way southwards from North Uist to South Uist, I drive across a ribbon of tarmac marked out with white lines in a sea of water and find myself gazing out at an almost entirely blue scene, from the gently slapping water at the base of the causeway to the deep blue sky at the very top of my windscreen. A sign says: *CAUTION: OTTERS CROSSING*, and a flock of birds oscillates off to my left. I have rarely seen a more idyllic seascape, which just goes to show how dramatically things can change here.

I was booked to stay at the Polochar Inn on the far south coast of South Uist that night, and found myself, as ever, short of time to get there. Again I had underestimated how much there would be to see and how much time I would spend chatting with local people about island life.

And so I didn't have much time for South Uist. Which is a shame. This is the sort of island that seems unremarkable at first but reveals itself to be rather magnificent over time. It is the sort of place where stone circles are hidden for centuries only to be revealed by a moorland fire, and where people were still making mattresses out of the abundant seaweed as late as the 1960s. Here regular high tides and storms throw seaweed and kelp onto the shore, attracting birds and providing unusual ingredients such as dulse, a type of seaweed often cooked in a broth.

I speed through the island, sadly missing turnings for lochside walks, smokehouses and a business called Hebridean Jewellery. I do, though, pull over at the birthplace of the woman who remains perhaps the most famous resident of the Outer Hebrides.

This is Flora MacDonald. Flora helped Bonnie Prince Charlie to escape from Scotland after Culloden, taking him by boat in June 1746 from Benbecula to Skye disguised as her servant, a so-called Betty Burke. She then secured him passage across to Raasay and on to France. He led the rest of his life in unexceptional safety; she ended up in prison for her troubles. But her legacy is in many respects far more positive than the prince's. Her mission, after all, was successful, and she later became a romantic hero for her part in the Jacobite cause. When she died in 1790 her funeral cortège is said to have been a mile long.

Flora's precise birthplace is up for debate but it is very likely to have been in one of the ruined blackhouses around the farm that now stands here at what was once Milton township. Today it's a quiet spot, an area of otherwise unexceptional farmland sitting between the Atlantic and the island's main spine road, the A865. The memorial cairn itself is a simple stone hump surrounded by a low wall; the sign that tells Flora's story is faded and pockmarked. For a woman of such legendary status it is somewhat disappointing.

The Polochar is the sort of inn you really want to find after a long day's drive: the type where simple food is served in the bar and you end up drinking with a local crofter.

I arrive just before sunset and so, after dumping my bag in my room, I make my way outside with a pint to sit on the wall of the car park and look out at the low humps of Barra across the sound. Sunsets are so phenomenal in the Outer Hebrides that a sundowner is becoming my daily ritual. It has become a recurring punctuation mark in my travels.

It had also become the gong for dinner. Because people eat exceptionally early in the Highlands and islands. Not normally one to book dinner for any time before 8pm, for weeks now I had found myself setting about my main course as others asked for the bill, and being the last lonely person chatting away to the staff as they wiped tables and cashed up around me.

So I had learned to eat as soon as it got dark, which turned out to be an even better plan here at the Polochar. This is because the seafood on the menu is hyperlocal and the scallops, hand-dived by Martin MacPhee off Barra and Eriskay just outside the front door, often run out.

"You're lucky," Neil tells me as he brings me my portion of scallops. "Yesterday we ran out and people were very unhappy. It's the most popular dish."

They are also absolutely massive. I order scallops with abandon wherever I can find them but these were something else: "The biggest I've ever seen," I tell Neil as he spins on his heel to return to the bar.

This stops him in his tracks. "Oh, these aren't that big," he says, as if I were quite mad. "They get as big as the top of your glass." That would be a pint glass, of course, roughly nine centimetres (more than three inches) across.

"I feel short-changed, in that case," I tell him with a smile.

I also order smoked salmon from the island's Salar Smokehouse, one of those places I missed out on earlier, and then retreat into the main bar hoping to find a lively local scene.

It turns out that the local scene is Roddy. Neil had appeared on the bar, the dining room had closed up behind me, and I was trying to override my not entirely irrational fear of talking to random men leaning on bars.

Life in the Outer Hebrides is different, though. Here people expect a chat, and Roddy tells me with bewildered indignation that "Some people who come here are so rude. They just come in for dinner and don't even talk to the local people."

Frankly I don't seem to have much choice, and so I see an opportunity to pepper somebody with my questions. I have been collecting Gaelic words I want to understand and start showing Roddy phrases on my phone, asking him to pronounce them. If this sounds like I was hounding the poor man, that may be true, but he seemed delighted to share his native language with me and tried to teach me longer and longer phrases as the evening wore on and I bought him another whisky.

Of course, being the organised and sensible journalist that I am, I noted down everything Roddy taught me in my phone's notes app. Only I failed to recognise that this would make no sense to me the next morning. Gaelic is a living, breathing language and often spellings of the same word vary from island to island, even person to person. Roddy had explained that some letters are missing in Gaelic's smaller alphabet so extra ones are used to make the right sound. This explains why to an English speaker Gaelic appears to have far too many letters, and trips us up with trying to pronounce them all. I feel a little better about struggling with the language and resolve to try harder.

The next morning I have a short wait for the ferry and some work to do, so I take a seat in the bar and ask Neil for a coffee. He asks where I'm off to today and I tell him I'm booked on the ferry to Barra. "Ah, the Devil's island," he says darkly. "They still eat your firstborn over there. And tourists." The rivalry of close neighbours, it seems, is the same everywhere.

After a rainy night, the day has dawned all grey skies and white caps out in the water. "It makes you feel really alive though, aye?" says Neil. "When it's wild and you can get outside in it, it's brilliant."

The ferry to Barra leaves from Eriskay, the neighbouring island reached by a causeway. This was the site of the sinking of the SS *Politician*, the whisky-laden ship that sank in 1941 and inspired the book – and later film – *Whisky Galore*.

Nothing seems to get people here more excited than the conspiracy theories that surround the wreck. Tall tales about the royal family and thousands of pounds' worth of Jamaican currency had flown around the bar last night, but the real question is where all the whisky ended up. "My uncle told me there are lots of bottles buried in the hills, but nobody knows where," Roddy had said. "He was one of the first people on board. Part of the rescue effort," he concluded with a wink.

Sadly, tall tales of the whisky-soaked weeks that followed the SS *Politician*'s watery end were all I had time for on Eriskay. I was off to Barra and I was very excited about it. I couldn't quite put my finger on why, beyond the fact that much of the seafood I had been eating seemed to be coming from there.

On my arrival Barra felt bigger than I had expected, and driving from end to end, from the ferry port to the main village of Castlebay, took me about twenty minutes. I had missed lunch at the Castlebay Hotel where I was staying and asked the woman on reception if there was anywhere to get lunch in the village. I was fully expecting her to say no, but instead she told me to go to "the toffee place".

The Hebridean Toffee Company had an extensive menu of hot food but no seating except a few tables outside – in the rain. I was already soaked and wondered briefly about eating my chicken wrap in the car. But then I remembered that I was in the Outer Hebrides and decided to see if the hotel might not mind if I sat somewhere, in a guest lounge perhaps, and ate my lunch if I ordered a drink.

Back at the hotel, no sooner have I uttered words to this effect than the woman serving on the bar is ushering me over to the best table, in the window looking out to sea, and saying that I needn't order a drink. I insist on having a ginger beer, and later she insists on taking my rubbish away for me. Nobody else comes into the bar while I'm sitting there, but nonetheless I'm pretty sure that most places I've visited in England would have sent me packing. I feel immediately that Barra is my kind of place.

I also find Castlebay instantly lovable. It feels a little like a toy town, somewhere where everybody rubs along very nicely together and the worst thing that ever happens is a few pieces of mail getting mixed up. The village has a hospital, a medical centre, a post office, a police station, a church, two large hotels and a decent selection of places to eat. It is like the perfect little town you would build in *SimCity*, and I cannot imagine a village its size on the mainland having such facilities. It even has a ferry service, the five-hour sailing across to Oban that I would be on a few days from now.

Castlebay is – you will no doubt be shocked to learn – named for the castle out in the bay. This is Kisimul Castle, the seat of the MacNeil Clan, and it stands on a low, rocky island surrounded entirely by the waters of the bay. Every half-hour a boat runs across from a small jetty in the village to the castle, and I decide to hop on one of the last of the day.

There isn't a whole lot to see at the castle. This isn't the sort of place where you tour the tapestries and discuss the cutlery; this is a castle for stalking around the battlements and looking out to sea as generations of powerful clan chiefs would have done. I stand in the rain and look out into the Atlantic, feeling far from stressful city life but not in the least bit remote. This has clearly long been a place of importance.

Castlebay was in fact once one of the world's most productive herring ports. Today there is a self-guided walk along the shore, following signs fixed to the tops of wooden barrels, which explain the history of the herring industry here. It was the fish merchant James Methuen who developed Castlebay's natural harbour into a herring port in 1869, and at the industry's peak more than six hundred boats fished from here. Curers set up curing stations around the harbour, at one time numbering more than forty, and a bank, hotel and shops were opened. The village's Catholic church was built to accommodate the influx of fishermen.

The remains of the curing stations can still be seen along the water's edge today. I pick out short strips of iron once part of railways and try to count how many stone pillars that would once have supported wooden jetties still pepper the coastline. It was the fish merchants working these stations who put pressure on the UK government to extend telegraph cables to the island in 1884, and the industry gave local women more opportunity – to travel as 'herring girls' as far afield as Great Yarmouth and Lowestoft in England. They returned with new ideas and an independent spirit.

With a nip now in the air, I retreat back to the bar at the hotel and ask for a gin and tonic. Recently a gin distillery has opened on Harris and I assume that this will be the most local gin I can order. "You know, we do have a Barra gin," the woman on the bar tells me. "It's distilled in London at the moment, but they're hoping to build a distillery here soon."

This, I am told, is made with carrageen seaweed, harvested by hand from around the coasts of Barra. Again I am struck by the entrepreneurial spirit of the Isles. It is easy to think that, because the Outer Hebrides are far from the cities of Glasgow and Edinburgh, they must be quiet, that nothing of interest could possibly be going on here. And yet I have found entirely the opposite – people who choose to make their lives on an island tend to be rather keen to do things for themselves. I feel like I have found my tribe.

For those who do want a taste of the city life, Barra is surprisingly well equipped to offer it. The island is home to one of the few airports in the Outer Hebrides, and it certainly is a memorable one. Because Barra Airport at Traigh Mhòr is the only one in the world where scheduled flights use the beach as a runway.

I couldn't imagine anything much more exhilarating than flying across the Minch to land on a beach, and so I had decided to do something rather nuts. I was taking a joyride to Glasgow, simply for the thrill of it. On my arrival at the airport I take a seat in the window overlooking the runway/beach. A sign says: *Beware of sand blast during aircraft movements.* Another reads: *No persons allowed beyond boundary fence when windsock is flying.* The Old Firm football match between Rangers and Celtic, currently underway in Glasgow, is on the radio, the coffee machine froths and hums in the background and a hubbub of chatter fills the room.

After about half an hour – there's no need to be at this airport two hours before take-off – an announcement is shouted across the café: "Air traffic estimates it'll be in at twenty to." This was the woman from the Loganair desk literally calling out across the café. No intercom system is necessary when all dozen or so passengers are sitting within a few metres of each other.

Over the next few minutes a blue van slopes out onto the beach to check the runway, scaring off the birds and making sure nobody is out for a walk or a paddle. It sedately performs a couple of loops of the beach and comes back, to be hosed down by about the most serene-looking airport worker I've ever seen. I'm pretty sure he is whistling.

Suddenly a plane appears from above the airport, its wheels reaching out towards the wide expanse of sands left behind by the retreating Atlantic. It touches down with a spray of damp sand and circles round to park up in front of the terminal. Within moments the door is flung open and the passengers are stepping off, exiting from beneath the wing and hanging around as long as they please, snapping pictures (the visitors) and bidding the two-person flight crew goodbye until next time (the locals).

Gradually, and without the jostling I've come to expect from people at airports, we all get up and make our way out of the door, flashing our boarding passes as we go. My seat is right up the front and I settle in as I normally do, clipping my seatbelt and gazing out of the window. I still can't quite believe that I am looking out at nothing but sand and water.

It is the co-pilot who talks us through the safety demonstration, leaning on the empty front-row seats to tell us about emergency exits as I watch the pilot clicking switches and talking into her headset. The cockpit is entirely open and so I am able to watch out of the front window as the plane's propellers power up and we race off across the sands. I feel the usual lift in my gut as we leave the ground, and look down to watch the waves pass beneath us, the sands scudding away behind us, the beach suddenly smaller, and then smaller still.

It is a magnificent flight, and with a cruising altitude of only about ten thousand feet (three thousand metres) I can make out Coll and Tiree, Mull and Iona as we fly above them. I can also see the pilot's instruments, clearly marking out the islands we are flying over when the clouds obscure the view from the window. It is like looking at a map spread out on the ground, and only makes me more keen to get to those islands I will miss on this whistle-stop tour.

The flight back is even more beguiling. There are fewer clouds later in the day and I can spot boats in the Minch as we cross back over the waters that separate the Outer Hebrides from the Inner Hebrides. On the cockpit instruments I can see Barra fast approaching, and watch out the window as its lumpen green hills and arching white beaches make their way up to meet us. We fly lower and lower above the water, as if we are in a seaplane and will land right here on the Atlantic swell.

But then, suddenly, we are just a few metres above the rippled sands, a vast expanse far wider than any airport runway I have ever seen. In every direction all is sand, and I watch our wheels reach ever downwards towards the beach, finally meeting it with a delicate thud. The propellers continue to spin, our wheels bump over the ridges in the sand and splash through the puddles of seawater that remain, and I have a massive grin on my face. I cannot imagine a more scenic flight.

CHAPTER ELEVEN

Mull and Iona

I arrived in Mull in the late afternoon, brooding Highland peaks standing ahead of me, shrouded in grey mist. A peach light strained from behind the hulk of the land, as if the sun was trying to break through one last time before sinking into the ocean.

Mull is a dramatic island, and I am instantly smitten. The island's famous capital, Tobermory, is a ridiculously attractive place, an ancient fishing village on the Sound of Mull, its harbourfront cottages painted in rainbow colours, mirrored in the harbour waters and backed by a protective cloak of mature trees. It is instantly recognisable from dozens of tourist posters, numerous travel websites and even children's television – it was the setting for the BBC's popular *Balamory* series.

But Mull is so much more than just one cute fishing village. The island has more than three hundred miles of coastline, for a start. Its highest point, Ben More, is the only Munro in the Hebrides outside Skye. And it is arguably the best place in the UK to spot golden eagles.

I have another destination in mind on my arrival, though, and am cutting straight through the heart of Mull to reach Fionnphort, the jumping-off point for Iona. I had expected a quiet journey but there is significantly more traffic than I have seen in any other place with single-track roads and I find I am pulling into passing places more regularly than usual. As the Hebrides go, Mull is one of the busier

On the drive I entertain myself by getting giddy about trees. Out in the Outer Hebrides there simply aren't very many of them, and I am delighted to return to driving through forest. Every landscape I have been looking at for the past couple of weeks has been uninterrupted by anything taller than waving grass or the odd clump of heather, and having something different to look at is a joy.

Iona has been a place of Christian pilgrimage for centuries and is considered by many people to be the most sacred place in Scotland. Getting there could certainly turn many a pilgrim to prayer, at least on the day of my crossing. This, Michael at the guesthouse has warned me, is "one of the most dangerous stretches of water in the British Isles". If you drew a line due west of here you wouldn't reach land until you hit Newfoundland. The full force of the Atlantic passes between Mull and Iona here, in a narrow channel. This makes the currents unpredictable, and on this wet and blustery day it makes even CalMac's sturdy vessel sway from side to side all the way over.

A gaggle of us, dressed in waterproof hiking gear and firmly pulled-on hats, has gathered by the ferry pier to watch the boat make its way across from Iona to pick us up. Here the ferry more or less runs back and forth all day, but an announcement has already been made several times: "We'll get you over but we can't guarantee we'll get you back."

"Are you going to risk it?" a woman in her sixties asks me above the rustle of her layers of purple and navy blue waterproofs. A worried look wrinkles her face as her husband stands staring out to sea behind her in bewildered disbelief. The dock creaks eerily.

"I'm booked overnight," I tell her, probably looking about as certain as her husband does that this is a good idea.

After boarding I withdraw, unusually, inside and begin to dry out my already sodden gloves on the radiator. It is wonderfully positioned right beneath the window, so I lean against it to watch our progress and hope that this won't be the warmest I will feel all day. At least, I figure, I have a room with central heating waiting over there for me; if the weather continues to be terrible I can always retreat inside. This thought keeps me smiling until I realise I have forgotten my book. I hope Iona will have enough to entertain me.

Being on Iona doesn't feel like being in Scotland. Religious places naturally attract a certain type of visitor, one which – fair enough – is here primarily because they believe. I was here to check out the scenery and perhaps have a pint or two in the pub afterwards. The other guests were here to share music and, I overheard several say, in American accents, "to feel the divine touch". I felt like I had somehow wandered into a religious retreat in some out-of-the-way US state.

I decide to head up the highest point, Dun I. My guidebook tells me that on a clear day you can see as far as Skye; the howling winds and heavy grey sky tell me otherwise. It's an easy walk, though, only reaching some 100 metres above sea level, and turns out to be a good way to get the lay of the land. From its blustery summit I look down on the island's abbey, so tiny between the pea-green fields and the churning sea, and pick out the main road that leads down to the beach where St Columba, who founded the monastery here, is said to have landed from Ireland in the sixth century. As I struggle to clear the hair from my face, I'm buffeted backwards by an Atlantic wind thick with misted seawater. With no hint of a clearer patch of sky to come I retreat down the muddy slopes to the village.

I spend the rest of the afternoon poking around the abbey and the village museum, which turn out to be great wet-weather activities. St Columba founded a monastery here in 563 and today the abbey stands quietly impressive in squat, chunky stone. Iona may not have the soaring architecture of the great Gothic abbeys of Melrose and St Andrews but it has a doughty presence, its cloisters and corridors filled with the daily conversation of running a religious centre.

There are many beliefs that find their genesis here at the abbey. It is where the Book of Kells, that famous illuminated manuscript, is thought to have been created. It has long been believed to be a gateway to the afterlife, and that being buried near the relics (remains) of St Columba means being nearer to God, with a shorter journey to Heaven. It is also said to be the birthplace of the Celtic cross, a design which adds a ring of stone around the crossing point to support longer and more ornate arms.

It is certainly a meaningful place to many, but it doesn't quite get into my soul the way I know it does for others. I struggle not to see opportunism in the story about Abbot Dominic Mackenzie, who asked the Pope to grant a 'special indulgence' that anyone visiting on the feast day of the 9th June would spend less time in Purgatory. Hundreds of people came and the money needed to rebuild the church was raised. Today people come to visit the abbey and so spend their money in the hotels and shops here. Their willingness to spend perhaps explains why a bottle of Rock Rose gin on sale in one shop was a whopping £55. It generally retails around £35. That also seems pretty opportunistic to me.

Personally, I found the Iona Heritage Museum far more inspiring. There are local stories aplenty in this one-room museum and I find myself absorbed for hours. It can be tempting to think that an island as small as Iona (only some three miles in length) would have few tales to tell, but this is far from true. I have always been fascinated by island life and find myself scribbling notes about the runrig system, where islanders drew lots for a share of the arable land, and about early ferry operations, when smoke would be raised on Mull to signal to the ferryman to come over.

Setting up life on a small rock in the Atlantic may be testing but since necessity is the mother of invention, island life is often very creative indeed.

Iona was quick to embrace tourism. As the era of steamship travel dawned, the island benefited almost immediately. It had some help from Samuel Johnson. He had visited Iona on his 1773 *Journey to the Western Islands of Scotland* and his resulting book had been a roaring success. People wanted to follow in his footsteps and discover this so-thought 'wild land'.

Johnson was rather more positive about Iona that I am feeling this morning, stepping onto a boat bound for Staffa with a certain amount of relief to be leaving. I am joining a cruise that is similar to the Sacred Isle Cruise that began here in the early nineteenth century. This was marketed as a circular trip out from Oban to Iona and Staffa, and much the same trip continues to run today. This morning I was booked to join one of Staffa Tours' boats in Iona, heading out to Staffa and the world-famous Fingal's Cave, before landing back on Mull.

This has been slightly tricky to organise. It is late in the year and trips are not running daily. My itinerary has been rejigged to accommodate this jaunt out to Staffa and I am looking forward to seeing the cave said to have inspired Mendelssohn's overture *The Hebrides*, and Turner's eponymous painting.

I had seen pictures of Fingal's Cave before. This is one of the iconic Scottish sights, after all, and its appearance is reminiscent of the Giant's Causeway in Northern Ireland just across the water. But those pictures are nothing compared to the real deal. Fingal's Cave is one of those works of nature that you can't quite believe isn't some sort of Hollywood special effect. The columns of basalt are just too uniform, too perfectly sculpted, to feel quite real. They look like a machine must have cut them to some sort of pattern, as if there might be a stencil hidden somewhere in the back of the cave, being used by human hands to force rock into hexagonal flutes.

The truth is far more explosive. These columns were formed by volcanic activity, when lava was expelled from the earth's core, cooled into a solid form and then contracted and fractured into the pattern we see today.

The island of Staffa is uninhabited and the only way to visit the cave is on an organised tour (unless of course you have your own yacht). I have joined Staffa Tours and find myself entirely alone for the initial crossing back to Mull from Iona. Sadly I haven't lucked out with a private tour; a coach has disgorged at the top of the harbour and a line-up of tourists stands waiting for us to tie up.

I have bagged a seat on the back deck of the boat and sit in the sunshine and sea spray as we speed northwards. The land around us is almost all Mull; we are in the wide inlet between the Ross of Mull peninsula in the south and the chunkier northern head of the island to the north. We are exposed to the Atlantic on one side, enveloped in Mull on the other.

It is a spectacular crossing to a spectacular island. On arrival we tie up at a tiny harbour at the base of the cliffs, the boat swaying as the two-man crew help everybody off by the elbow. It is a slow-moving line up the steep rocky steps and I decide to opt out where the route divides, heading for the smooth, grassy ground on the roof of the island. Almost everybody else continues on the path along the cliffs to the cave, and for a few brief moments it seems as if I have the island to myself.

All is flat atop Staffa, a bit like standing on the top of a layer of Victoria sponge that is waiting to be iced and joined to its partner. In every direction there are islands, peninsulas, indeterminate swathes of land that could be either. I am certain I can see Skye. Then less certain. Then certain again. In the Hebrides it is often hard to tell what is mainland and what is island, and it is easy to see how this mattered very little to our seafaring ancestors – when you travel by water, who cares if where you are heading is or isn't attached to a larger chunk of land?

It is beautiful up here but I am on Staffa to see the cave, so as the crowds on top thicken I head against the tide, back down the steps and along the cliff path. Although a metal handrail has been bolted to the rock and the areas between columns filled in with some form of concrete in places, largely the walk out to the cave is along the hexagonal columns and is every bit as dramatic as walking the Giant's Causeway. I spring from hexagon to hexagon, imagining them as stepping stones and grinning like a child at play. Few coastal walks can be this entertaining – and no other walk I have done has ever led me to quite such an arresting cave.

Fingal's Cave is unforgettable. I challenge anyone to be underwhelmed here, or to pass up the "Wow" that comes to the lips on seeing inside the cave for the first time. At the entrance, some of the columns reach from the ground right up to the cave roof, a concertina of basalt that looks like an accordion extended, or, more aptly, the pleats of a kilt. In front of these sit shorter columns, their tops as sheer as if they have seen the slice of a samurai sword. The roof above is triangular, shaped like the gables of a house, and the water rushes in and out at the base, a cobalt blue turned white by the churn. It is possible to pick your way along into the mouth of the cave, peering into the darkness at its back many metres away and still as neatly divided into those pleated rocks.

Back at the harbour the water has kicked up a bit and the boat coming back to collect us seems tinier than before. I spot thick yellow ponchos on the seats outside and realise this crossing will be a bit bouncier than the one over here. We are told to sit inside if we don't want to get wet. I am eager to ask whether that could indeed have been Skye earlier and so I head to the wheelhouse, poking my head inside and asking if I can chat to the crew for a minute or two.

The boat is swinging from side to side a fair bit and so I am taken by the elbow once again. I find my footing and, being careful not to lean on anything that looks in any way important, hold my own as the Atlantic tries to toss the three of us into each other. I ask if I could have seen Skye from the trig point on Staffa. The guy not currently driving the boat instantly says, "No." Then, almost as suddenly, he looks up into the corner of the wheelhouse, holding his chin, almost comically in thought. "You'd be able to see Coll and Tiree, but Skye…"

I seem to have hit on something, and he begins pointing out of the window at various hulks of land on the horizon. "It could have been Rùm," he says, as the horizon sweeps from the bottom of the window to the top and back again. At about this moment I almost bang into the guy who is actually trying to steer us home and so we all decide (well, they do) that having me standing there trying to figure out the lay of the land isn't such a grand plan. I head back to my seat with the promise that we will all look at a map later on.

Sure enough, just after docking back on Iona, my friend from the wheelhouse pops up with a map. Almost everybody has left to spend their allotted three hours on Iona before returning to Mull and back to Oban. And so, on a pleasant crossing back to Fionnphort, we chat over the map and which Hebrides we have and haven't been to. Coll and Tiree, I tell him, have alluded me so far and will continue to on this trip. "Well, you have to leave something to come back for," he says, folding up the map. He's right, of course, but I am already yearning for more time in the Isles.

On my way back across Mull, en route to Tobermory, I spot a brown signpost for a scenic route. At the end of a long day and with darkness fast approaching, this is not the time for a detour, however beautiful it may be. And so I decide, with a somewhat heavy heart, to stick to the main road, the more prosaic A849.

The road snakes on through Glen More. Ahead and all around me, sage and russet peaks stand glaring down at the road, man's tiny and ultimately meaningless intrusion. As the mountains close in on the road, waterfalls cascade down the banks at the roadside like ribbons. Carpets of fern blanket the space in between one peak and the next, and the road weaves its way across ancient stone bridges, as perfectly shaped as the ones you might get with a model railway set. *Yeah*, I think to myself with a grin, *this isn't scenic at all.*

I arrive in Tobermory in the evening, excited for my brief visit. Because Tobermory is home to the most famous – and, in my opinion, the best – pub in the whole of the Isles, the Mishnish. The Mish sits in canary yellow on the harbourfront and if it's singing then all is right with the world. This is the sort of pub that you pop into for a pint before dinner and end up leaving, countless hours and whiskies later, singing 'Flower of Scotland' to yourself with someone else's scarf around your shoulders, and having met someone who may or may not have once been on *Pop Idol*. After a night at the Mish, Tobermory looks even more idyllic.

It is all down to the harbour. Tobermory was founded by the British Society for Encouraging Fisheries because of its natural harbour, and it is the ever-revolving community of fishermen and sailors that makes the Mish such a raucous place to spend an evening. With Oban so close across the water, though, Tobermory was never a huge commercial success and so today it has been saved from the ravages of industrialisation and been able to retain its low-rise cottage-strung frontage and hinterland of greenery.

That hinterland tempts me out around the island's north the next day, eager to blow away the hangover and see a medieval fort, a Gothic castle and an extinct volcano – all within a few miles of the village.

I drive out to 'S Airde Beinn first, the highest point on the rim of an extinct volcano that is now filled by a crater lake. The parking is beside a ruined cottage, the path a barely distinct track up through the boggy forest following a stream. It is soggy going but doesn't take too long and I soon find myself emerging, gently sweating and with water seeping up my legs, at a gap in the crater's rim. Water a deep navy blue fills the landscape in front of me, a doughnut of scrubby grassland rearing up around it. To the west

I find myself looking out to Coll once more – she seems to be forever tempting me, chiding me for not including her in this itinerary. Fortunately to the north is the recognisable stump of lava on the Small Isle of Eigg, An Sgùrr. This is a lump I plan to be standing atop just a few days from now.

I spend the rest of the day happily driving around Mull's north. I stop at Glengorm Castle for an easy three-mile walk out to Dun Ara medieval fort. This ancient stronghold now sits largely forgotten in a field, but on my approach the foundations are clearly visible, and the site of an old harbour is easy to pick out over to my left. I clamber up the narrow gully that holds the path to the top and find myself standing on the summit of a rocky outcrop enclosed by a man-made wall. This was clearly an important place at one point but today it is just me and one white-tailed eagle showing any interest. And even I am more interested in the view, trying to work out whether the dramatic land mass I can see across the Sound of Mull is the Ardnamurchan peninsula or the Morvern. There is always the promise of more out across the water.

CHAPTER TWELVE

Glen Coe and the Great Glen

It was a delight to be back in Oban. I've spent many nights here, waiting for ferries or about to embark on a cruise around the Isles, but this was a fleeting visit, and, as if the town knew I was on the clock, she put on quite a show. The sun was warm, enough that I took off my coat and actually basked.

One of my favourite places in the world to eat seafood is right on the pier here, alongside the CalMac ferries pulling in and pushing off. It is a place generally referred to as 'the seafood shack', a green-painted shed where a local father-and-son team dish up the daily catch. I order a dish of buttery scallops and dig in on the quayside, their juices running down my fingers.

Oban has long been a tourist haunt but it is the sort of place where there is very little to actually see. And so you spend your time eating seafood, strolling along the water and drinking whisky in the pubs. There are outdoor stores for stocking up on walking socks and the like, and a distillery to while away a few minutes chatting about whisky. But that's really about it, and I am always delighted to feel like all I must do here is enjoy myself.

One thing I had taken to doing when I was particularly enjoying a place or just generally having a good day was buying a postcard and sending it to a friend. About twenty friends and family members were regularly receiving postcards from me by this point in my trip, and in response I would often receive a video of a child shouting, "Thank you!" while holding up a train picture in their fists, or a picture-message joke from a desk-bound friend highlighting the contrast between my days and theirs.

Choosing the cards and writing the two or three paragraphs it takes to fill them was making me think about my experiences and edit them down into bite-size memories, and it was helping me to share my trip with the people I missed back home. For me social media can never replace the one-to-one contact and closeness I felt in these moments. Feeling connected is priceless.

So it was ironic that one postcard-receiving friend sent me a link to a news story while I was sitting in a pub in Oban writing my next batch. It was the story of Britain's oldest postcard publisher, J. Salmon, shutting up shop. A lack of demand, they said. It seems that the wider British public does not share my joy of sending a postcard to a loved one. And what an awful shame that is. Still, I suppose we still have Instagram.

From Oban I am heading for Mallaig. Much like Oban, Mallaig is the sort of place you only visit when you're en route to somewhere else, and I am heading for the town because it is the jumping-off point for Eigg, where I have an overnight stay booked and plans to climb An Sgùrr.

The drive out to Mallaig takes me across Rannoch Moor. It has been several weeks since I walked at the other edge of the moor on that squelchy stroll out from Rannoch Station, and I had forgotten just how unforgiving this landscape is. The straight road requires little focus on steering and so I gaze out onto the moorland, stretching endlessly in chocolate brown on either side of my wheels. Birds of prey are doing circles above the waterlogged landscape and I can imagine that, should I step out of my car and strike off into the bog, I will never be seen again.

This landscape has claimed many lives over the years, perhaps most famously in Glen Coe. This is the mountain pass between the moor and the sea and it is about the most dramatic landscape it is possible to imagine. Coming from the south, you first encounter Buachaille Etive Mòr and Beinn a'Chrùlaiste, one either side of the glen, each one utterly terrifying. They stand like gateposts, hulking great ones, suggesting that perhaps you might turn back now, to more bucolic lands and safer pastures.

But continue you must, because this is one of Scotland's greatest drives. The A82 through Glen Coe transports you across the pass and through a geology lesson. I had seen a video that explained how Glen Coe had been formed and now as I stared up at its buttresses this autoplayed on my mind's screen. I can almost hear the tectonic plates crashing together and scraping up into these dramatic, raked peaks. All is dark as I drive, the clouds shuddering across the landscape in vast swathes of charcoal grey, the raindrops pelting from the sky mottling my windscreen and slowing me to crawling pace.

It is easy to see how this landscape has claimed lives. Not least those of the MacDonalds of Glen Coe, massacred here in their own lands by the Campbells, their long-standing neighbour and enemy. This was not a simple clash of clans; this was a massacre ordered by the Secretary of State.

The MacDonalds here were constantly fighting their neighbouring clans over their penchant for raiding, pillaging and cattle rustling. After King William of Orange ascended to the throne in London there remained much support in Scotland for the deposed Stuart king, James VII. This was the change in monarchy that ultimately led to Culloden, but at this time

England was at war with France and King William sought only an oath of allegiance from the clan chiefs.

Unfortunately for MacIain, the chief of the clan, there was a deadline for this oath, and he missed it. Bad weather, the need for a distant sheriff to witness the oath, and his capture by the Campbells were to blame, but John Dalrymple, the Secretary of State, had always hated the MacDonalds and so took his opportunity. He ordered that the clan be "cut off root and branch". Nobody under seventy was to be spared.

And so, on the 13th February 1692 during a howling blizzard, Campbell soldiers – despite having received traditional Highland hospitality in the MacDonald homes for a full twelve days beforehand – set about killing every man, woman and child. The next morning thirty-eight MacDonalds, including MacIain himself, were dead. Many more escaped into the hills, only to perish in the white-out conditions.

Despite murder being somewhat normal in those days, the massacre outraged the country and the Campbells were seen as barbarous for many years, if not centuries, afterwards. A sign at the Clachaig Inn, in the heart of the glen, still says: *No Campbells*. I am not 100% sure that this is entirely a joke.

The weather was continuing to close in and I was starting to wonder about my trip out to Eigg the next day. At my hotel in Arisaig that evening the wind was howling down the chimney and although I knew Eigg lay just offshore, the thick clouds obscured her from me entirely. My CalMac app was telling me that the routes in the Small Isles were on yellow alert, and those words from the other day on Iona – "We can get you over but we can't guarantee we'll get you back" – rang in my ears.

I was due to spend the night on Eigg but couldn't shake the thought that the ferry the following day might be cancelled, leaving me stuck over there. If I went it would be on foot; the car and all the armoury of long-term travel (my clothes, my books, my emergency supplies) would remain on the mainland. Perhaps thoughts of being stranded on an island might have seemed romantic if I'd been travelling with someone, but the idea of being all alone in a youth hostel with no restaurant on site, no way of getting anywhere and possibly no phone signal filled me with dread. And besides, I was meant to be on Skye a few days from now. As I tucked myself up in bed that night I resolved not to travel – the risk just wasn't worth it.

Opening the curtains the next morning I am surprised to see Eigg offshore – and blue sky. Suddenly a trip there is back on the cards. Except that I have got up too late, and CalMac are still on yellow alert. I realise that I could throw on my walking trews and drive round to the ferry terminal, but those thoughts of getting stranded on an island with (very) limited accommodation, food and entertainment, without the car and on my own in the rain and wind, get the better of me.

But then, as I approach the centre of Mallaig in search of breakfast, I see CalMac pushing out to sea, the waves breaking on her bow. My immediate thought is: *Damn, I should have been on that.* But then the break in the clouds closes, CalMac disappears behind a veil of grey, and the rain throws itself with the force of a lorry passing at my windscreen.

Although this is clearly not my time to go to Eigg, I am frustrated not to have made it over there. Travelling at speed means travelling to the easiest-to-reach areas – those with main roads and regular ferry connections – and I wish I had more time to take on the trickier journeys and those that simply take longer. Though at least this has provided me with yet another reason to return.

One place that I was able to go back to as a result of missing Eigg is Glen Coe, and I was delighted to be able to bag a room at the Clachaig Inn for the night. This meant plenty of time to explore the glen itself – and to visit the Glenfinnan Monument en route.

Although many people think that the Glenfinnan Monument

is a figure of Bonnie Prince Charlie, the man standing atop the eighteen-metre-high stone pillar is in fact a Highland soldier, and a tribute to those who fought on the prince's behalf. It was built in 1815, and an inscription attached to the wall reads: *On this spot, where Prince Charles Edward Stuart first raised his standard.* Historians now believe that the standard was raised on higher ground on the other side of the road, but no matter; it's a beautiful spot to remember those who gave their lives for the Jacobite cause. Some of the Scots pines that stand here could well be old enough to have witnessed the raising of that flag in 1745.

Glenfinnan is also an official Harry Potter film location, the *Hogwarts Express* having chugged over the viaduct here in both *Harry Potter and the Chamber of Secrets* and *Harry Potter and the Prisoner of Azkaban.* And so the largest crowd of people in the museum and shop was standing in front of three stands selling Harry Potter paraphernalia. This excitement means that the National Trust can now sell a Gryffindor pen for £26 or a wand from the so-called 'Noble Collection' for £32. The shop is larger than the exhibition.

Which is a shame, because the exhibition is really quite good. It has clearly been redone quite recently, and there are interactive displays focused on how people showed their secret support for the Jacobite king. Some would carry miniature portraits, or wear jewellery with secret symbols – a rose for the king, rosebuds for his sons. Some people wore a white ribbon to mark the king's birthday, and those feeling bold might toast the king 'over the water', while he was exiled in France. One display features a metal jug on a shelf, on which, when you hold a reflective board underneath it, a back-to-front phrase in support of the king overseas is revealed. I find myself quite engaged with this and start thinking of other ways to pass secret messages, remembering the invisible ink I had as a child.

Those same high winds that have stopped me from getting over to Eigg have also closed the monument itself (you can normally go up it), and so I drive on, back into Glen Coe. As I enter the glen, I find that the scenery has been rendered even more sodden than the day before by the ceaseless rain. Waterfalls that would be a major attraction in other countries, England included, simply gush past the side of the road as if they were merely a drain. Which, of course, they are.

The main sight in the glen itself is probably the Three Sisters. Yet somehow I hadn't really heard of this hulking massif until now. I had not allowed any time at all for Glen Coe on my itinerary when I first outlined it, in fact, and standing here, looking up at this mass of towering mountains, I am at a total loss as to why on earth this could have been.

I blame my guidebook, which barely mentions them, and suddenly am not sorry at all that I haven't got to Eigg. Instead I stand and watch countless waterfalls unfurl down the dark olive slopes, jumping off them in bursts of white water as smooth slope crumples down into rocky crag. Wispy clouds obscure the ridge in parts, as if a rubber has been taken to a drawing but not quite managed to erase either shape or colour. Apart from a line of trees along the mountain's thick base it seems as though no life could cling on up there.

A walk in Glen Coe is not to be taken lightly, but there is one easy stroll I was confident of undertaking. This is the walk to Signal Rock through An Torr woodland. The National Trust bought this woodland in 1993, purchasing it from the Forestry Commission who were growing non-native Sitka spruce and larch. Gradually the National Trust is returning the woodland to its natural state, felling the spruce and larch and planting native species including hazel, ash, rowan, Scots pine, alder and birch. Felled trunks and lumber might line the path as I walk today, but the trust promise butterflies, woodpeckers, bluebells and wood anemones – as well as perhaps the odd badger – once the native woodland is back in business.

Signal Rock itself is surrounded by trees. This may well sound obvious but the interpretive panel here talked of gorgeous views along the glen and a history that suggested this may have been used as a lookout. I can't help but think that I can't see the glen for the trees, then grown inwardly at myself for this lame joke. Missing regular company, I fear I am starting to annoy myself.

An Torr and Signal Rock are close to the National Trust's visitor centre and I am keen to check out the exhibition here. It costs me £6.50 for the privilege. So now let me save you enough money for a drink or two by telling you not to bother. This museum isn't going to tell you anything you can't read up on in advance on the internet, and anyway, you've come to Glen Coe to be outside, not to fanny around indoors watching videos.

Videos, sadly, are what this exhibition largely consists of. There is one rather basic one on the geology of the area, one on ice climbing and one about the massacre that is so loud I can't tune it out at all. Reading the displays around it is quite literally impossible, the words in my head drowned out by those being flung at me from the screen. To cap it all, many of the inevitable touchscreens aren't working.

But perhaps I am getting grumpy. I have been on the road for weeks now and I am getting tired. Nothing is ever 'normal' on the road and I am starting to tire of it. On my car's satnav screen it tells me that it is learning my usual routes. Then underneath it says: *No regular routes.* I sigh when I see it this time I get back in the car, and wonder if I can keep going.

But then, the Clachaig. The day is drawing to a close as I arrive, and the pub's bright lights are burning in the otherwise ceaseless darkness of Glen Coe. As I step through the front door I am greeted with a warm fug of air, peppered ever so slightly with the smell of beer, and a cheery hello from behind the desk. Staying still here awhile suddenly seems a very attractive prospect.

Questions about where I've come from, what I've seen and why I'm here come thick and fast and all good-natured. The Clachaig is one of Scotland's most famous pubs and it didn't get its reputation for bonhomie by letting people check in without a good old blether first. I am shown to my room and told the Wi-Fi probably won't stretch this far, but that the lounge bar has a strong signal and that there's local ale on tap. I am back downstairs immediately.

I spend a couple of hours catching up on emails and drinking a pint or two from the Loch Lomond Brewery. There are several families staying at the hotel and for them it is already dinner time. They can only eat here in the lounge bar but for me the Boots Bar is calling – an over-eighteens, proper pub that is legendary for its atmosphere.

I am not disappointed. The bar itself lines one full wall of the room, supported by a long row of barrels and strong enough to lean on. The tables are also all wooden, the floor rough slate. *There is nothing to trouble a muddy hiking boot here*, it seems to say; *put your feet where you like and pull up a pew.*

I take a seat on one of the low benches and tuck into haggis, neeps and tatties in front of the smouldering fire. The clack of pool balls on the table behind me punctuates the chatter that fills the place; well-used Ordnance Survey maps are laid out with a crackle on the tables. I try the pub's own whisky and get my map out to plan the next day's touring. I don't think many evenings I have spent in my own company have passed quite so happily. My grumpiness is long forgotten.

One thing I was still slightly miffed about was not being able to climb Ben Nevis. It was simply too late in the year for someone of my limited experience and there was no way I was heading up Britain's highest mountain alone. English poet Keats climbed Ben Nevis in 1818 and is said to have compared the walk to "mounting ten St Paul's without the convenience of staircases".[35] And St Paul's, of course, is indoors.

But the weather had improved greatly and as I drove into Fort William, although it was still raining, a rainbow was now arching its way across the sky above Loch Linnhe. The sun was coming out and, arriving in sunshine after several days of rain and getting out of the car at Neptune's Staircase, it was all rather handsome.

Neptune's Staircase is a flight of locks on the Caledonian Canal. Not those natural bodies of water called lochs, you understand, but the pairs of gates on a canal that allow boats to pass up or down a hill by adjusting the water level in one direction or the other.

Growing up in Devizes I had spent many a childhood afternoon wandering up to the locks of the Kennet & Avon Canal to 'help' people push open or pull shut the heavy wooden gates, and waving to canal boaters who had been lucky enough to get the job of pushing the tiller rather than their back muscles. I love locks because they remind me of childhood and of home.

They are also, of course, a marvellous feat of engineering, and this flight is yet another work of the ubiquitous Thomas Telford. It is the longest staircase lock flight in Britain and allows access to the canal that ultimately links the Irish Sea to the North Sea. It also provides some of the very best views of Ben Nevis.

Sadly, my warm first impression of Fort William was not to last. Because, oh dear, what a disappointment it is. Few towns in Scotland have a more potentially gorgeous natural setting, but this has been almost defiantly squandered. A dual carriageway loops its way around the town, cutting it off from the waters of the loch and wrapping it in grey tarmac and concrete. Arriving here by car is to arrive in a fug of stress, and I began my time in Fort William circling McDonald's and Morrisons and peering through the rain at the endless dark blue 'P' (for parking) signs in search of somewhere to leave the car.

This was all thanks to the Alexandra Hotel, who had promised free parking but failed to deliver. Fort William seems to have been designed with the idea that everyone would come in by train, and the station is indeed well used. Sadly, so is the road network, and there simply isn't enough parking here for the amount of people visiting. The hotel car park is chock-a-block.

If you don't know the town, it also isn't all that obvious how to get in and out of the centre from the dual carriageway. Especially in the rain, with increased traffic on the roads and a windscreen the wipers were struggling to keep clear. And so I find myself funnelled back out onto the duel carriageway, following those 'P' signs and heading in precisely the wrong direction, the hotel disappearing behind me.

The first car park I can find that will let me leave my car overnight is behind Lidl and, naturally, lacking a functioning payment machine. After feeding brand-new pound coins into an angry little metallic slot for about a minute, the rain seeping down my neck, I realise that the council have probably not yet roused themselves from their offices to change the machine to accept the new coins. But – aha! – there's an app for that.

Back in the car I download the app, fill out a registration form that asks for a password including an upper-case letter and one Sanskrit character, discover I have already registered, bang my head on the steering wheel, tap in every password I can think of ever having had and, success, I am in. Then I just have to update my credit-card details, tap in a code which meant craning my head out of the window to see with a squint the miserable little numbers written on the car park sign, and pay £2.40 for the privilege of it all. I am, it is fair to say, not immediately loving Fort William.

Let's not focus on the grumpy walk with my baggage I then took through the car parks and underpasses of Fort William to reach a hotel that can best be described as mediocre. Let us turn instead to the wonderful West Highland Museum, which focuses on the history of the – you've guessed it – western Highlands of Scotland. This is a fascinating region whichever way you look at it, and when that way is through well-designed exhibits in a welcoming, friendly – and free – museum, then it is a fabulous way to spend an afternoon.

I spend a long time in the very first room, one which tells the story of the Commandos. After Britain's army was crippled in

France, evacuating men but little else from Dunkirk, Churchill ordered the setting up of an elite fighting force, something that had never existed before. These were the Commandos, and their training centre was at Achnacarry, just north up the Great Glen from Fort William, and the seat of Clan Cameron. The "wild mountains and remote glens" to the west of the Great Glen were seen as the ideal training ground for testing physical fitness and mental resilience. By the end of World War II, twenty-five thousand men had passed through the training centre here.

It's worth visiting Fort William to check out this museum, but something else that is perhaps disappointing about the town itself is that there is no fort. I'm certain that I'm not the only person who, on their first visit to the town, expects to see some sort of fortification. A few walls strung around the High Street, perhaps, or an out-of-town ruin commanding fine views over the surrounding countryside. The museum tells me that some sections of wall remain at "the roundabout near Morrisons" but there really isn't much to see, and the same display also tells me that much of the disused fort "was destroyed to make way for the railway line that came to town in 1894".

The railway continues to dominate the town today, but the fort that played a significant role in the Jacobite Rising of 1745 is now but a memory. It lives on in the Gaelic name for the town – An Gearasdan, which means 'the garrison' – but in little else. It is hard to believe that the fort the Duke of Cumberland is said to have described as being the only Highland fort "of any consequence" was ever here at all.

Fort William today is a crossroads. This is the meeting point of several A roads including the Road to the Isles, as well as the Caledonian Canal, the West Highland Way footpath and the West Highland railway line. On any tour of the western Highlands it is nigh on impossible to avoid Fort William, even if I might have liked to.

Fortunately, my second night here was to be spent at a rather wonderful B&B, and I am delighted to check in to The Grange and dump the car. My room has a teeny terrace with views of the loch and my host, Joan, is only too happy to book my dinner for me that night at the lochside Crannog Seafood Restaurant while I dash back out to the train station.

I am booked to spend the day on *The Jacobite*, a vintage steam train that departs Fort William daily for the round trip to Mallaig – and the chance to cross the famous 'Harry Potter viaduct'. This, it turns out, is the main draw for the majority of my companions. Our carriage of six consists of me, a couple from Kent in England, and a trio from Australia. That trio have booked this trip entirely for its Harry Potter credentials. They are in their mid twenties and on a whistle-stop tour of Europe that seems to have allowed about three days in Scotland. And yet this is one of their highlights. Which perhaps explains why their trip to the buffet car results in them happily spilling snacks and drinks out across the table, including several boxes of Bertie Bott's Every Flavour Beans that cost £4 a pop. The box lists dirt, earthworm and bogey as flavours.

They share the spoils around (I avoid those beans) and chat animatedly about Harry Potter and the sights we are going to see. At a point that means nothing in particular to the rest of us, the woman sitting opposite me leaps up and screeches, "This is the Harry Potter bit!" We weren't yet at the viaduct – this was a view over the loch somewhere near Arienskill – but presumably it has featured in one of the films at some point. I watch her dangle her phone out of the window at an alarming angle and snap away.

We spend much of the rest of the journey to Glenfinnan chatting about our travels. Just after we have all agreed that Fort William was indeed a bit of a let-down the train suddenly slows to a halt, the wheels gently shrieking as they slide along the tracks. An announcement comes over the tannoy: "We've just stopped here briefly to pick up a phone someone dropped two days ago." We laugh in recognition at how easily this could have occurred again today. And then: "We also just need to stop a bit further along to retrieve the driver's hat. It blew off when he was looking for the phone." There are raised eyebrows all round as we all – at least I imagine – silently wonder at how much trouble was taken to retrieve somebody's easily replaceable possession.

There really is nothing like a steam train, and as we start up again the gush of the steam, the peep of the whistle, that chugging noise that drops its beat ever faster as you pull away along the tracks, has me smiling. There is also wine for sale and a gorgeous view from the window. I settle happily into my seat and bask in the joy of having company for the day.

The highlight of the journey is, of course, Glenfinnan Viaduct, and as we approach, it seems this is the highlight of more people's day than just those of us on the train. Across the hillsides stand dozens of people, in small bunches and in pairs, holding up cameras and phones and waiting for the train to pass by. Part of me wishes I was out there with them, watching the steam train pass across the three-hundred-and-eighty-metre-long viaduct, its puff of silvery steam billowing out behind it. From inside the train there isn't much to photograph, but I did feel a little like a celebrity – I've never been waved at so much in my life.

When I wake up at my B&B the next morning it is to a view of the water and the hills beyond. I had left the blinds open, wanting to wake up to beauty, and I am delighted with what I see when I open my eyes. Fort William is beginning to look a whole lot better.

Between the thick foliage that stands between me and the loch I can see the slick grey-blue of the water, rippling only slightly. Behind it stand the hills, where the green tufts of trees are clumped together like heads of broccoli, filling the lower slopes. Behind them stands an even higher mountain, more severe, denuded of trees and glowing slightly purple in the sunrise. It takes me a while to realise that two hills are in fact three, the definition only picked out as the sun rises higher and illuminates the indent between them. I look down for a moment at my cup of tea and, looking back, all has changed, the colours washing out more and more as the sun rises. The sky beyond retains a blush of red from the early hour but looks like it doesn't, for the first time in days, yield rain.

This is perfect timing, because I have only a day or two to see the Great Glen, with a detour to Loch Ness before turning west once again for Skye – and it is all so much better in the sunshine.

Loch Ness is over twenty-two miles long. It has an average depth of 130 metres and holds the greatest volume of water of any lake or loch in Britain. It fills the northern half of the Great Glen. And yet the main thing anybody wants to talk about is Nessie, the mythical beast who is said to live in the loch's waters.

The Nessie legend started with St Columba in 595 when he allegedly came across a monster attacking a man and used prayer to save him. This tale is related in *Life of St Columba*, a biography written by the ninth Abbot of Iona, Adomnán, a distant relation of the saint. You'll forgive me, then, for being sceptical, since the same work – and let me state this again, written by a relation – also tells of him controlling sea storms and raising the dead.

This is how legends are born, and they continue with grainy pictures that could easily have been doctored and model monsters made for films that later sank and appeared in future photos. As with all legends, though, the only way to be sure one way or another would be to prove it to be true. We can't, after all, prove categorically that Nessie does not exist and so, presumably, she will continue to.

Most Nessie sightings are said to have been from Urquhart Castle and so I head to the castle to see if I can spot anything out there in those waters myself. An otter, perhaps. The castle is another Historic Environment Scotland site and certainly one of my favourites, commanding a ridiculously glorious position on the shores of the loch and standing proud amid the scenery. A castle is about the only thing I can imagine competing with the mountains of the Great Glen, rearing up to the heavens from either side of the water, and Urquhart Castle is a cracker, its battlements standing sturdy after raid upon raid and year upon year.

The castle fills a rocky promontory in the very heart of the glen and during its five hundred years as a medieval fortress it was the subject of great conflict. It passed from the Scottish to the English and back again many times, including being taken by the notorious Edward I, so-called Hammer of the Scots, in 1296. Up until the 1500s it was also a target for the Lords of the Isles, rulers of the semi-autonomous Kingdom of the Western Isles, who were seeking to expand their kingdom and their influence. During the Jacobite Rising government forces used Urquhart as a garrison; when they left in 1692 they blew it up. This beauty has certainly been ravaged.

She is gorgeous, though, and it is still possible to climb the stairs of the Grant Tower and gaze down over the battlements to the waters beyond. I stand here for several minutes, willing Nessie to appear. A young girl pops up behind me instead. She turns to her mother: "Mummy, is this where Nessie lives?" she asks.

Her mother and I look at each other and smile. "Yes," she answers. Because, after all, there's no harm in a little bit of legend.

CHAPTER THIRTEEN

Skye

I had decided to sneak up on Skye from behind. This is the most popular of the Hebrides, and most people visiting it arrive by driving over the bridge from the Kyle of Lochalsh on the main road. Aside from its epically awesome scenery, it is this ferry-free link to the mainland that has made Skye such a draw. For most, the certainty of a bridge crossing trumps the romance of a ferry crossing every time. Also, of course, it is free.

Seeking romance, I had decided to take the ferry across the Glenelg Straits. There has been a car ferry here since 1934, but as a crossing point it has been in use for far longer. That's because Glenelg is the point on the mainland that lies closest to the island, and for centuries cattle were driven into the water here, forced to swim across the straits on their way to market.

Today you won't see a cow poking its head above the waterline. But you will see the MV *Glenachulish* – the only remaining manually operated turntable ferry in the world. What a privilege it is to be able to travel on her.

As I drive down to the ferry, the young woman in charge of

loading and unloading the *Glenachulish* is motioning at me with two raised arms, an indifferent look on her face as she sees me eyeing up the steep, shelving slipway. Keen to appear as nonchalant as she does, I let the car roll downwards, bumping up across the thick metal gangplank onto the car deck, at this moment turned at a ninety-degree angle to the rest of the ferry. I am the only passenger for this crossing, so park surrounded by space copious enough to keep even me completely cool, and get out of the car to wonder at this fantastic piece of engineering.

The majority of the crossing seems to consist of the woman pushing the platform around and untying the ropes that hold us against the slipway – there simply isn't that much water to cross. Some six hundred metres away Skye rears up beyond the churning water, all brooding dark purple slopes and tumbling low cloud. A seal pops up in the straits to see what's going on, and a stiff breeze lifts my hair from my collar. It is exhilarating.

What's more, the sense of arrival docking at Kylerhea is far more exciting than any I have felt on previous trips to the island. The Skye Bridge may well have the slender, sloping look of ultra-modern design – and it does give you the thrill of driving above the water and swooping down on the island – but the Glenelg ferry has true romance. That bridge, after all, isn't the only one of its type on the planet.

And then there's the road from Kylerhea, a rollercoaster in tarmac. As I press down hard on the accelerator, the windscreen is entirely sky, the bonnet pointing up so vertically that it feels like it could tip over backwards and send me tumbling back to the slipway. At the top I feel like I am teetering, and I imagine cartoon legs running in thin air. For a second it runs through my head – *What if there's no road over the hill?* – but of course there is and the next second I am tipping forwards, straight onto the brake with my stomach still up on that hilltop. The brakes groan softly with the effort of it all, and I am tempted to do the same. It's like riding tarmac waves, and I'm glad to reach the main road across the island.

Skye has become the one Hebride that everyone is determined to tick off. Unfortunately, there is a tendency to try and do it in a day and at my B&B, Hillstone Lodge, one of the first things Russell, my Glaswegian host, tells me is of the couple who travelled from Glasgow for just a one-night stay, simply to eat at the Three Chimneys.

Now, the Three Chimneys is a fabulous restaurant and well worth travelling for, but it is fifty miles from the bridge and a five-hours-plus drive from Glasgow. That is an awfully long time to spend in the car for a few – admittedly wonderful – plates of local seafood.

Food on Skye is generally excellent, but it is the scenery that draws the bulk of the crowds – and that warrants a much longer stay. Because Skye is a truly show-stopping island. Of the 282 Munros in Scotland, twelve of them are here on Skye and eleven are in the island's Cuillin Ridge alone. So many towering peaks in such a compact space makes for the sort of toothy scenery that has people using words like 'foreboding' in relation to a geographical feature. Though, of course, up there on the roof of Skye, plenty of bad things can indeed happen. I have no intention of testing my mountaineering skills with any of Skye's tough Munros.

I do, however, intend to explore the island more fully than I have been able to before, and so set off on my first full day for Portree, the island's capital. Portree has the sort of pretty harbour that makes for a great postcard shot and although it isn't quite Tobermory it does exude a quiet charm, its pastel-painted cottages lined up along the harbour wall below the hills.

I decide to pop into the Visit Scotland office here. Partly, it has to be said, to avoid the rain. Since there aren't many people around, after I have stocked up on leaflets to attractions I won't possibly have time to visit on this trip, I ask the woman on the till if Skye has been particularly busy this year. "Aye, it has," she says with an audible sigh of delight. "We saw it coming last year. We had our busiest season, but I reckon this year has been busier.

And we've just had a film crew here, filming for the new Robert the Bruce movie."

Skye also appeared as the backdrop to much of the 2015 film *Macbeth* starring Michael Fassbender, and I raise my eyebrows at the prospect of even more tourists coming. "Ah, the locals don't mind," I am told with a smile; "it's good for the economy. It's parking and toilets that are the issue. People aren't going into the cafés so we need public toilets. Hopefully we'll get the upgrades we need."

Out on the Trotternish Peninsula I see the problem immediately. This is Skye's crowning glory, a peninsula of world-class scenery that has appeared on screen in blockbuster films, Visit Scotland ads and thousands of Instagram feeds. Probably the most famous sight is the Old Man of Storr, a basalt spear of rock that clings on like the last man standing on the exposed Trotternish Ridge, formed by a giant landslip that has left behind a bizarre landscape of collapsed hills and craggy cliffs. You barely shake off Portree before the Old Man rears into view and his associated traffic starts to clog the roads.

On a dreich and windy Sunday in autumn there are plenty of cars pulled up at the roadside – on any available muddy patch that looks even vaguely flat and accommodating. The tarmacked parking area is packed with cars and campers, and coach-sized groups in inappropriate clothing are climbing down in their dozens from their tour buses. The wind is blowing the rain in swarms of droplets across the landscape and over the road, great, blustery plumes of water covering every exposed feature, human beings included. I fight my way into my waterproof trousers and exit the car, only to be quite literally blown into the info cairn at the walk's start. I turn back immediately, and still people are setting off to walk up to the Old Man on a day when nobody should be walking anywhere so exposed. Least of all people wearing leggings and Converse trainers.

I decide to drive on a bit further, to Mealt Falls. The waterfall is raging today, crashing off from the clifftop down towards the sea and covering my face in droplets of close-to-freezing water. In the distance I can see Kilt Rock, a formation of basalt columns that crumples the cliff edge like the pleats of a kilt and rests on a chunky sandstone bluff that slopes down to the water like a hoof. The weather is keeping most people back from the cliffs but I still have to park on the mud at the side of the car park; even on a crappy-weather day there isn't enough provision for the number of visitors here. It must be a real stramash in high summer.

Things improve at the Quiraing, where driving on a bit further than others are willing to means I can find a spot to park. The view might not be quite the classic shot I have seen all over Scotland on postcard stands but it is the same landscape, different for one glorious reason – that I have it entirely to myself. Water gushes beneath the boggy ground underfoot, the wind whistles gently in my ears and I remember what my guide Mitch told me on my first visit here: "Look the other way; the landscape is just as impressive."

The Quiraing is one of those places you simply can't get sick of. You could visit dozens of times and every time you would see something different. This is a landscape for walking in and taking all day about it, not whizzing through on a coach, seeing only what can be seen through a window and stopping where you are told to.

I am happy to remember the walk I took with Mitch on that previous trip, hiking up through emerald grassland to reach the top of the Quiraing's inland cliffs and look down over a landscape that looks like a geology model made to teach students what happens when a landslip occurs. Below my feet had been a view of an almost flat green expanse, sitting slumped in the middle of a harsh grey land mass, as if the whole thing were made of ice and had begun to melt from underneath the centre, pulling the top down into the middle and leaving a few hardy edges.

It is awe-inspiring, a rousing landscape that puts me automatically in a good mood. I find I am standing there looking down over it once again with a grin on my face. I have long loved Skye but this time I am determined to truly see it, away from the crowds and with nothing at all to spoil my view.

Skye is a huge island, slightly larger than Hertfordshire and almost three times the size of the Isle of Man. As a result, it is mercifully easy to escape other people and, since my accommodation is on the Duirinish Peninsula in Skye's far west, I am staying well away from the crowds.

I am close, though, to Neist Point, and several people, Russell included, have told me that I must take the walk out to the lighthouse here, an easy walk of about a mile each way along an undulating concrete path. This turns out to be excellent advice, because it proves to be one of my favourite short walks of my entire tour of Scotland.

It starts in the rain, but as I walk down the steep-stepped path, taking hold of the handrail in extreme gusts of wind, the precipitation stops and I am able to put down my hood. Before this moment my eyes had been fixed dead ahead, but now I can look in every direction – and it is magnificent.

Ahead of me a chunk of land set in the water like the resting head of a hammer rises up between the leaden waters of the Minch and the washed-out silver of the sky. Like a watercolour painting, the sky is all brushstrokes, in every shade of grey from off-white to pewter, and just visible on the horizon are the dark lumps of the Outer Hebrides.

They tease me as I descend into the saddle between the main island and the chunky outcrop I am heading for, disappearing behind the darkest clouds at times, at others confusing me. First they convince me that I am looking at Harris, before equally convincing me that, no, I am certainly looking at North Uist.

Turning in the other direction I look along the west coast of Skye, its towering cliffs marked by the odd plunging waterfall, catching the sun in an otherwise dark hulk of landscape. There may not be the bizarre basalt formations of Trotternish here but there is still plenty of drama. A buzzard swoops overhead; otherwise I have it all to myself.

The Lighthouse Board, I am told, renovated the actual lighthouse quite recently, but the other buildings – which would have been the keepers' cottages – are slowly falling to rack and ruin. There are warning signs telling me to keep out of the buildings themselves but I can see through the windows, where net curtains hang, tied and yellowing.

But I am not here to see the lighthouse; I am here to take in the view. Out here on the edge of land it is mostly of the sky, stretching from above my head to the low horizon like a duvet pulled taut, one that has aged and fallen into lumps so that, in looking through it, some patches are opaque while others let through the light. I am certain now that I am looking at Harris, the lumps on the horizon too pronounced to be anywhere else, and I wonder if I am staring back at An Clisham, ironically able to see her better from here than I had been able to up close.

Part of me wishes I was back out there in the Outer Hebrides. But then I remember that I am still on an island here, and that, despite the bridge and the crowds, there is still very much the feeling of island life, the sense of the sea all around me, that I have grown to love.

This side of Skye has plenty more to explore, too, including the beach at Claigan, better known to most as coral beach. Claigan has been winking at me across the water ever since I arrived at the B&B, and I am told – by more than one excited local – that only a few weeks earlier a film crew had built a village here as part of the shooting of that Robert the Bruce movie. In that case, this is sure to become a popular spot and I am delighted to get here on a day when hardly anyone else has ventured out this far.

The walk to the beach is more than a mile each way but I am happy to bound along the path, crossing the boggiest areas on the stepping stones laid out along it and looking across Loch

Dunvegan to scan the hillside for my B&B. I reach a pebbly beach first, strung out along the shoreline in a great arc, but for the coral beaches the path continues, through a gap in a drystone wall and across an almost imperceptible rise.

As I reach the top, suddenly the beaches are quite startlingly obvious, a great sweep of buttery yellow in an otherwise entirely green-and-blue landscape. In the distance are the Harris hills again, as well as a flat-topped, protruding headland that must surely be joined to Skye and looks a little like a battleship cruising into view. It is crunchy underfoot here, as the wee coral shells snap beneath my boots. The black rocks that dot the beach are hairy with seaweed, the darkest possible contrast to the shock of bright yellow sand. It is unlike any other beach I have seen in Scotland, and again I have it all to myself. I suddenly realise that I have not seen a single coach all day. This could be a different island to the one I saw yesterday.

The next morning I was leaving Hillstone Lodge and what had started to feel like my Skye family of Russell, Patrice and their dog Inca. As I packed up the car I asked Russell for his surname, and the answer came back: McSporran.

Now, Scottish people are – at least in my experience – a dry and witty bunch who love a deadpan joke. And so I am convinced that he is winding me up. I turn with a raised eyebrow and a chuckle. "Now that's a joke, surely," I say.

Far from causing offence, this seems to endear me to him further: "Ah, you've been in Scotland too long," he laughs. "Most English people nod politely and say, 'That sounds very Scottish'; people in Glasgow think I'm pulling their leg."

Of course I could never be too long in Scotland, and my few days with Russell, Patrice and Inca have restored my love of being on the road to boot. I am driving onwards, and back to the mainland, with a smile on my face. Not least because first I have planned a stop at Talisker Distillery.

Talisker has long been one of my favourite whiskies. I love its strong flavour, its ability to transport me back to Scotland from any London pub. And so I have decided to do the distillery tour here despite Islay – Scotland's whisky island and home to a whopping eight distilleries – fast approaching on my itinerary.

The Talisker Distillery is a classic Scottish whisky house, low-slung on the lochside, painted in brilliant white, with a slate-grey roof and a slender silver chimney. It sits on the shores of Loch Harport, and from here there are views of the Cuillin, dark and jagged in the background.

The tour itself is much the same as it would be at any other whisky distillery, with information about malting and fermentation thrown at us as we stroll around the stills and the mash tuns. The beginning of the process is much like beer making, with the barley malted and added to water taken from the spring behind the distillery before being fermented with yeast. These are the only three ingredients – it is the distillation process that makes each whisky different.

"Every distillery has distinct stills," our guide, Gordon, tells us. "In Speyside the stills are taller and thinner because they're going for a floral taste. Talisker is all about the fire." That fire comes from a longer S-bend in the wash stills, which gives the mix more time in contact with the copper. This is what makes Talisker different, and so tasty.

Naturally on my way out I sample a wee dram of the Talisker 10, the distillery's peppery mainstay. I am careful only to sip and not to sup; I have to drive after all. I pick up a bottle of the distillery release – only available here – and stash it in the car for later.

I am delighted to be taking a taste of Skye with me, and even happier that I have been able to leave time for one final stop on the island that has wormed its way into my heart as my favourite Scottish isle. This will be the Fairy Pools, a spot that is second only to the wilds of Trotternish in the Skye popularity stakes.

Here I find I am back to being part of the crowd, and there is nowhere available in the car park proper to leave my car. Instead I must park on very rough ground at the roadside. I am heart-stoppingly close to a teetering edge, the sort that even the most modern car's sensors cannot detect, and so I find myself clinging to the steering wheel and peering through the windscreen, justifiably terrified that I might well drive straight off the edge. I wish I had a passenger to wave me into this space.

As I strike off along the footpath in yet more rain, I pass couples and families returning to the car park. Unlike on almost every other walk I have taken in Scotland, nobody says hello as I pass. I wonder how busy a walk has to get before people stop greeting each other, a custom that I have long suspected is more about ensuring someone might later stop to help you if you get into difficulty than it is about being friendly.

Whatever the motive, I've always liked the camaraderie of the hiking set and I find myself grumbling under my breath at how people here seem to be ranging over the landscape like a pest. I count at least fifteen people with tripods, many of them extended to well over half my height, and find myself constantly dodging past people taking photographs. I doubt that there can there be an original picture to take here, especially in today's grey conditions, and wish that the photographers blocking the path would at least acknowledge the walkers picking their way past them.

But nothing can detract from the beauty of this place. The pools are a cascading series of pristine waterholes along the River Brittle. Each one is as clear as ice and, I am told, about as cold. This is a popular wild swimming spot in the summer but today I cannot imagine much that would be more uncomfortable than plunging beneath these waters.

The appeal of a swim here is obvious, though. Even on this chilly, cloudy afternoon. The Cuillin stands as an insurmountable wall ahead of me, the waters seemingly spilling straight from its vertiginous slopes. As they fall they are sheerest white, like a bridal veil unfurling, and as they pool in each placid puddle they turn seemingly to glass, the brim a mirror reflecting back the mountains. I struggle to think of a more captivating landscape. Yes, Skye is definitely my favourite Scottish island.

As if Skye didn't have enough to recommend it, to reach it by road almost everyone passes what could be said to be Scotland's most picturesque castle. Eilean Donan sits where three sea lochs meet: Loch Long, Loch Duich and Loch Alsh. This was a strategic location when it was built in the thirteenth century and today it remains so, though for a different reason. I can hardly imagine a better location for holding sway over tourists and parting them from their cash.

This is about as photogenic a spot as you can imagine for a castle. Eilean Donan sits on an island surrounded by water, reached by a triple-arched bridge in solid stone. In every direction the tranquil waters reflect the hills of the Highlands, and across Loch Alsh the razor ridge of the Cuillin signals its final farewell. On a late-autumn afternoon there is a bluish hue to it all, like a filter placed over a lens. The colours in the landscape feel bleached, as if they are fading from view, and it feels as if winter is coming, the beginnings of its frosty embrace starting to grip.

Eilean Donan was originally built as a defensive measure against the Vikings. She stood the test of time but was no match for the English when it came to their anger at the Jacobite Rebellion. The castle was garrisoned in 1719 by forty-six Spanish soldiers who were supporters of the Jacobite cause. They had stockpiled more than three hundred barrels of gunpowder and were awaiting a delivery from Spain of weapons and cannons, when the English got wind of their plans for an uprising and laid siege to the castle. Although Eilean Donan held out for three days – some of its walls were more than four metres thick – the Spanish soldiers were ultimately overwhelmed and surrendered. The English turned the gunpowder on the castle, blowing up what they had not already destroyed.

The castle sat in sad though presumably rather charming

ruins, cut off from the mainland, for the next two centuries. Then, in 1911, Lieutenant Colonel John MacRae-Gilstrap bought the island and dedicated two decades to rebuilding the castle – and securing for himself the title of Constable of Eilean Donan.

He succeeded by 1932, and it seems unlikely that more than a handful of today's visitors suspect they are visiting a twentieth-century construction and not a medieval castle. No matter – for me the charm of Eilean Donan is the location rather than the stonework, and I spend a happy hour or so poking around the battlements and watching the weather pass over the water.

With time getting short I only have time for the briefest of coffee stops in Plockton. This charming village had captivated me on my very first visit several years ago – and it wasn't just the pretty harbourfront and palm trees that did it. I had arrived mid afternoon, and the kitchen at the Plockton Hotel was closed. I had heard of the legendary Plockton prawns – as large as langoustines, I had been told – and was desperate to try them. I asked if food was being served and, despite the negative answer, stayed for a drink. I mentioned in passing that I had heard about the prawns and was an ardent lover of shellfish, before taking a seat in a corner overlooking the water.

No sooner had I settled in than a plate of prawns appeared in front of me. "Well, we couldn't have you coming to Plockton and being disappointed," the woman who was tending bar – and who, I assume, had popped into the kitchen to prepare the prawns – said with a smile. I left with the tang of shellfish on my fingers and an unshakeable love for Plockton.

Even more legendary than Plockton and its prawns is Applecross, my destination for the night. I had only to cross the Bealach na Bà, or Pass of the Cattle, to get there. This is the third-highest road in Britain, reaching 626 metres above sea level. A sign at the turn-off from the main road tells me that I can expect gradients of one in five, and hairpin bends. It also declares that it is "not advised for learner drivers".

I soon see why. The first mile or so of this single-track road is no more taxing than any other Highland road I have driven. But then you reach the first switchback and it's a white-knuckle drive from there on out.

I find the switchbacks harder to tackle uphill, knowing that I must keep my foot on the gas enough to stop myself stalling, but terrified of popping over a crest in the hill to find myself nose to nose with someone coming the other way. I take the drive slowly, gathering traffic as I wend my way upwards above the landscape.

As I make progress upwards I relax a little. I have become used to passing places and manoeuvring the car into tight spaces on the edges of hills, and most people are driving at an equally cautious pace. I have learned to indicate into the passing places if I want someone from behind to overtake me and let a van and a nippy red car get past me, determined not to feel rushed by the prospect of holding up the local plumber or nurse.

Suddenly the landscape opens up and I find myself at the top of the pass. All at once I am heading downwards, my foot now firmly on the brake as I swing the steering wheel from left to right at each switchback. The road has mellowed slightly, the bends softer, and now that I am able to see the road ahead I can be sure that nobody is coming. I begin to enjoy the journey, sweeping down the hillside into Applecross exhilarated by a challenge completed.

And what a view there is in reward. Applecross sits across from Skye and the island is laid out before me, the Cuillin dominating the space between sea and sky. The sun is beginning to dip and has disappeared behind a long, low cloud. Its light is diffused in orange and yellow across the sky and through the ripples of the water. Despite the chill I take a seat on one of the picnic tables outside the Applecross Inn and raise a dram to the island across the water.

CHAPTER FOURTEEN

South to Islay

One of Scotland's mountains is a little, well, different from all the rest. Not because a castle has been built atop it, or a ski resort, but because it has been hollowed out.

The sturdy rock of Ben Cruachan was dug out from 1959 to 1965 in order to put a power station inside it. This sounds like just the sort of thing Dr Evil would do if he wanted to build a new lair. In fact it was the brainchild of a chap called Sir Edward MacColl, an engineer from Dumbarton who worked for the North of Scotland Hydro-Electric Board.

Ben Cruachan was the world's first reversible pumped-storage hydro scheme. This means that during the night water is pumped up from Loch Awe at the mountain's base to a reservoir at the top. It is stored there until the National Grid needs a boost of power – when everyone switches their kettles on at the end of *Strictly Come Dancing*, for example – and then allowed to flow back downhill through the turbines to produce electricity. Since power is cheaper during times of low demand, what is used overnight to pump the water up costs very little, and the power generated during the day can be sold at peak times at – you've guessed it – higher cost.

The best thing about Ben Cruachan, though, is that you can visit it. Throughout the day buses take groups of visitors along the thousand-metre-long tunnel into the guts of the mountain to have a gander at the vast machines that have the capacity to restart the National Grid. Our guide chats away as he drives the bus inside the Munro: "This is the largest pumped-storage power station in Scotland and one of only four in Britain," he says. Stats and numbers fly at us thick and fast from then onwards: Ben Cruachan is the highest point in Argyll at 1,126 metres. The reservoir can hold ten million cubic litres of water. Its catchment area is almost nine square miles and it gets some 15–20% of its replenishment from the rain. The staircase in the cable shaft is 1,420 steps, making it the tallest in Britain.

The stats are impressive but it is the sheer scale of the thing that has me awestruck. We have travelled into a cavern at the mountain's centre that is high enough to house the Tower of London. We are kept in a sort of glass-box viewing chamber, the turbine hall unveiled to us by the slow ascent of a screen – and it is incredible. Four huge, bright yellow turbines stand in a line, their shape reminiscent of a super-sized mash tun, their size hard to comprehend beyond feeling pretty certain that I could comfortably drive my car into one. Even taking into account my dodgy parking skills.

Our guide is telling us that this was all buried to save the landscape from being blighted. I'm sure most people wouldn't exactly be thrilled to find a series of almost neon-bright cylinders appearing on the hillside across from their house, and Ben Cruachan has saved this fine landscape from becoming an industrial monument. It is a Scottish success story, though sadly MacColl didn't live to see it finished, and later the whole thing was sold off by infamous asset-stripper Margaret Thatcher. Still, it can produce electricity from a dead start in two minutes – so at least we are safe in the knowledge that the National Grid will never let us down when we want to make a cup of tea.

I had stopped at Ben Cruachan on my way south to Inveraray. This is the traditional county town of Argyll, the vast and sprawling area of peninsulas and islands that stretches from just west of Glasgow all the way out to Kintyre, Islay and Mull. This is said to roughly correspond with the lands of the ancient kingdom of Dál Riata.

Inveraray itself is the seat of the Duke of Argyll, the head of Clan Campbell. The title is currently held by a man named Torquhil, who also happens to be the captain of Scotland's national elephant polo team. And if that sounds strange for a country not exactly known for its herds of roaming pachyderms then it might come as some surprise that Scotland won both the 2004 and 2005 World Elephant Polo Association World Championships.

This also makes Inveraray sound rather exciting and, unfortunately, it doesn't quite manage to live up to the status it presumably once had. The Duke of Argyll's castle remains here, but much of the original settlement is no more, cleared to make way for that castle and its beautifully landscaped grounds in the eighteenth century. The new town that was built to replace it is trim, pretty and homogenous.

It is also home to one of the best preserved nineteenth-century jails in the world, still standing with its courtroom complex on the shores of Loch Fyne. It is really quite an absorbing place to visit, reimagined as a living museum where actors greet you as you enter the jail cells and an audiovisual presentation sees life-sized mannequins in the courtroom tried for their crimes and read their sentences. It is both creepy and engaging all in one go.

This is the sort of place where you can put your child in thumbscrews and whip your best friend without reproach, and there are plenty of people monkeying around with the props left out for demonstration. I have a go at turning the crank machine, a heavy metal handle that turned cups through sand in a barrel for no reason at all, and find I am exhausted within about a minute. Yes, my arm muscles are as puny as a child's but I can't imagine that anybody could have kept this up for the demanded six hours without going quite mad. Which was, of course, the point. The threat of a stint on this would certainly have kept me in line.

Inveraray may have been the most important settlement in Argyll for some centuries now, but long before Clan Campbell built their castle here, a hill some thirty miles south-west was the capital of a kingdom that stretched as far afield as present-day Ireland.

This kingdom, Dál Riata, is said to have been founded around the year 500 by Celtic immigrants from Ireland. It was a Gaelic kingdom that had its capital at Dunadd, a mound in Kilmartin Glen that sits surrounded by the bogland of Moine Mhòr on a series of natural terraces. I am determined to stand atop this fort, which Historic Environment Scotland say was the royal power centre from about the year 500 to 800.

A serious collection of weaponry and metalwork has been discovered here, the sort of thing that only a high-status person would have, while the pottery fragments dug up point to far-reaching connections as distant as France and the Mediterranean. Today it feels like a remote spot, far from the cities and towns of modern life, but 1,500 years ago this would have been the heart of a community, one that – a sign at the site tells me – would have been able to feast on exotic foods and expensive wines.

The walk up to the fort starts in what looks like someone's back garden. I follow the path around the back of a neat whitewashed home and am soon snaking upwards, above the bogland. Suddenly the landscape has the touch of man; the stony path leading onwards between ancient rocky ramparts, chunky boulders that are slowly being separated from their neighbours by grass and purple foxgloves.

I have been sheltered by a sort of rift in the hillside and suddenly find myself out in the open, my hair swiftly wiped from my face by a gust. A map mounted on a board points to traces of buildings, their straight lines all that really gives them away, and the site of the ancient citadel, a flat area right up on top of the hill.

I am most interested in finding one particular stone, though. This is the Inauguration Stone, a rock that has a footprint-sized depression carved into it. It sits flat on the hilltop, commanding views over Argyll and out to the islands of Jura and Arran, and is said to have been the place where the kings of Dál Riata were crowned. Putting your foot into this carving meant domination of the lands around you. Naturally I spend a few minutes snapping pictures of my foot in that hole, though I'm not sure my grubby grey hiking trainer quite lives up to my newfound status.

It is not just Dunadd that marks out this area as one of Scotland's most historically important. The entire glen is packed with rock art, standing stones and cairns. I am standing at the heart of the greatest concentration of prehistoric stone carvings, Neolithic and Bronze Age monuments in the country, and there is plenty more to see.

Unfortunately I haven't allowed all that much time to see it and so I head straight for the Kilmartin Museum to get an overview and find out what the highlights might be. If the woman on the till is bemused by my desire to cram everything into about an hour she doesn't show it, instead pulling out a paper map and underlining what she feels I must see.

Once I tell her that I've already been to Dunadd, this pretty much amounts to the museum itself and Temple Wood Stone Circle. I have always enjoyed getting out into a historic site far more than simply reading about it and so I dispense rather swiftly with the museum, checking out the Bronze Age pots before slipping out quietly so it isn't obvious that I have spent so little time in here.

It's less than a mile up the road to Temple Wood but I drive the part I can to save time. This means skipping several cairns and I realise that I could easily have spent half a day here, tracing the lines of rock carvings and walking from one monument to the next, soaking up the feeling of the landscape.

This is, in fact, what I would suggest you do should you visit. Though if, like me, you're speeding south to the whisky isle I can heartily back up the woman from the museum's recommendation – Temple Wood Stone Circle is an atmospheric site and you can lay your palm on several rather impressive standing stones en route from the car park. These are part of Nether Largie, an X-shaped monument that some believe is aligned to where the moon rises and sets at certain key points in its cycle. As ever, we do not know if this is why these stones stand here, but I am starting to think that one of the joys of the prehistoric is that everything is somewhat shrouded in mystery. It is an invitation to the imagination.

I had been longing to get to Islay. And so I am delighted to pull up to Kennacraig Ferry Port and check in for the two-hour crossing. It's raining pretty hard and with the wipers turned off, the windscreen is as opaque as bubble glass. From the corner of my eye I observe a lorry backing onto the ferry. Chuckling to myself with relief that I won't have to perform this manoeuvre, I continue scribbling in my notebook and scanning the Islay map in my guidebook to see how many of the distilleries I might be able to weave together in my itinerary.

Despite having a reputation for cracking whisky that reaches around the globe, Islay sees far fewer visitors than Skye or Mull and so I am in a queue of only a couple of dozen cars, their engines gradually sputtering to life as their turn comes to back onto the ferry. A flutter of anxiety flickers in me as I realise this is what they're doing. It's not just the lorry that has been asked to spin around and drive backwards up the ferry ramp, it turns out; it's everyone. *What happened to roll-on/roll-off?* I panic as I crawl to the front of the queue.

Sometimes, though, you only have to observe someone else cocking something up entirely to realise that it really isn't that big a deal. And the man in the car in front of me was doing precisely that, his dark blue Volvo backing up at an alarming obtuse angle and heading straight for the Atlantic. I sat so long waiting for him to straighten up and inch his way onto the ferry that my engine shut off to conserve fuel.

Once the Volvo is finally in line with the other cars, the man in CalMac high-vis who is directing drivers onto the ferry approaches my window with a wave of the hand. He gives me that look of shared derision us Brits use when we have shared someone else's stupidity; a sort of raised eyebrow, aghast smile and a barely perceptible shake of the head. "You can't possibly do any worse than that," he says, beckoning me backwards. Feeling confident that this is indeed the case, I back the car on in a dead-straight, perfect line. I feel like swinging my keys around my finger as I walk away.

We arrive in Port Askaig that afternoon in the pouring rain. Opposite this small village on the Sound of Islay sits Jura, a wild island that appears only wilder on this grey day as I look across the Sound of Islay at her. The west coast of Jura harbours no roads, no communities and some of the most mountainous scenery in the Isles. Looking out from Argyll westwards it is almost impossible to find a view that does not include the Paps of Jura, three rounded, steep-sided mountains that all stand above 730 metres high. I have been staring Jura in the Paps for several days now.

I will not have time to set foot on Jura on this visit but on a previous trip I did sail through the strait between Jura's northern tip and the neighbouring isle of Scarba. This is known as the Gulf of Corryvreckan and, when in full flow, it is one of the world's largest whirlpools and one of the most dangerous stretches of water in the British Isles. I remember standing a safe distance away on deck as foaming circles formed on the water like the eye of a storm on a weather map. Other patches were unnervingly calm, as smooth as the top of a well-iced cake as the currents pulled the water taut above them. It is remarkable how calm the waters can be, so close to such chaos.

These waters are not to be messed with, and they nearly lost the world the wonderful *Nineteen Eighty-Four*. George Orwell was staying on Jura while in the midst of writing his most famous work and decided to take a boat out into the Corryvreckan with his family. His son later said that his father got the tide table wrong and so the boat capsized, tipping everybody out. Nobody was wearing a lifejacket. Since the whirlpool's highest waves have been reported at more than nine metres high, they were extremely lucky to survive.

I have more leisurely pursuits in mind today and so begin to make my way across the island on the only main road out of Port Askaig. There is nothing west of Islay until America and nothing south until Ireland, and yet every time I round a corner I seem to see land across the water. I rack my brains to remember what other islands would sit close enough to be visible.

On consulting the map, I realise that this is in fact all Islay, the strange hook-shaped island tricking me into thinking that her furthest reaches, the peninsulas of the Rhinns and the Oa, are not joined onto her at all. Because Islay is so spread out I have chosen to stay at what amounts to the island's crossroads, at Bridgend and the eponymous hotel. This won't put me near to anywhere as such, but it will mean that everywhere is about as winding a drive away as anywhere else.

I am keen, of course, to get to those whisky distilleries, but first I want to see the seat of the MacDonalds, Lords of the Isles. This is at Finlaggan, just off the main road between Port Askaig and Bridgend, and it sits on the loch of the same name.

Finlaggan was once the headquarters of the most powerful group for many miles around. The Lords of the Isles controlled not just the Hebrides, but mainland Argyll and the Glens of Antrim in Northern Ireland to boot. At the height of their power their territory even reached far up the Great Glen towards Inverness. They controlled the western seaboard of what is now Scotland from the twelfth to the fifteenth century and for most of that time they pretty much did what they pleased. Royal decrees from Edinburgh would have held little sway here.

And so I was expecting a fortified hill of some sort, a towering natural outcrop that stands high above the landscape, easily secured and ready to repel invaders. But this is Islay – a relatively low-lying island of fertile fields and few trees – and Finlaggan is entirely exposed. Walking from the car park I can see straight down to the loch. The landscape offers no natural protection at all. Which either means this area was so prosperous nobody wanted to challenge the status quo, or that the Lords of the Isles were so terrifying that nobody dared to. Possibly, of course, both these things are true.

In the loch at Finlaggan are three islands. Eilean Mòr, or large island, is joined to the mainland by a series of wooden duckboards, and stepping across the reed beds here I find the chapel. Very little of the stone walls remains, but the gravestones that lie here have been protected from the elements by panels of thick Perspex. At least one of the stones is small enough to almost certainly be a child's, and I read that the Lords of the Isles often buried their wives and children here at Finlaggan. They themselves were buried on Iona.

Also on Eilean Mòr would have been the Great Hall. I imagine the great, raucous banquets I've seen on screen in *Outlander* and try to conjure up an image of this island being at the centre of a world. I shut my eyes and for a second or two I can see children running around long tables, adults talking over plates of food and flagons of drink. Then a tweeting bird sings above the scene in my mind and my eyes open onto an empty, quiet landscape that is all grass and stone and water.

Islay's peace is not shattered by the intrusion of mass tourism. Here there are no huge hotels large enough for coach parties, and so big groups simply don't come. My hotel has only eleven rooms but is still one of the island's largest. Apart from when the whisky festival is on, visitor numbers are small. Agriculture remains the main industry.

I am certainly getting the personal touch on my stay at the Bridgend Hotel. I am trying to get a taxi to take me over to Port Charlotte for dinner but I don't have any phone signal. I enlist the help of the front desk, and find I have started quite the search. The woman on reception leaps straight into action when I ask, and yet finding a taxi proves difficult. As I stand there, feeling more and more like an imposition, two more staff appear and yet more phone calls are made. Every taxi driver is referred to by their first name: "I've tried Jim." "What about Hugey?" "Have you tried Carol?" Eventually it's decided that Jim can fit me in if I'm happy to come back at 10.30pm, and three beaming faces smile from behind the desk at me, mission accomplished. I almost feel like I should invite them all to dinner, though I'm not sure Jim's cab could take it.

It is worth the trip to Port Charlotte. Partly for the wonderful dinner of local venison at the hotel and partly because this is the village most people agree is the island's prettiest, its sparkling whitewashed cottages arranged around a sandy cove that overlooks Loch Indaal. It was built in the 1820s to house the workers of the long-defunct Lochindaal Distillery. These were people who had left their lives of crofting for a life in industry, and it seems unlikely that they saw the wee cottages here in quite the same rosy way most of us do today. They were, after all, forced into this new way of life when the landowner's desire for more profitable sheep farming took their homes from them. The cottages may be pretty but they weren't the homes they had built for themselves – and whisky making shares little with crofting.

Whisky making on Islay has a hefty pedigree and the island has long been producing single malts that taste nothing like those made elsewhere. Here there is a unique ingredient, a maritime peat that has formed from the very guts of the ocean – the seaweed and the crustaceans – and been washed and sprayed with salt water for centuries. This gives the whisky produced here a smoky, rich, kick-in-the-throat quality that captured my taste buds long ago and pulls me up short every time I think I might fall in love with a Speyside.

I love the whiskies made by Kilchoman, the island's smallest and newest distillery, but the distillery sits alone on the west coast of the island. A better day's whisky touring can be done in the island's south, where the big hitters of Ardbeg, Lagavulin and Laphroaig sit in a string along the coast outside Port Ellen. Three distilleries in as many miles. From the outside, each one looks more or less the same: a low-slung bleach-white building on the waterfront. If their names weren't imprinted, in bold black letters as tall as me, along their sides I don't believe I could tell them apart.

Laphroaig is the closest distillery to the village and so I make it my first stop. I find a slick operation, the shop lined with the white tubes their whiskies are sold in. There is plenty of merchandise too, from clothing to water jugs, and the tours you can do include peat cutting and a four-and-a-half-hour 'water-to-whisky experience'. Quality is everything here, with the barley still malted by hand and the peat still cut using elbow grease, and I wish I had the time to have a go myself. I settle for a tasting of the quarter-cask, a whisky matured in smaller casks for more contact with the oak and a softer finish.

A new path has been cut alongside the main road between the three distilleries and so I can walk safely onwards to Lagavulin, the distillery that makes my go-to whisky, Lagavulin 16. By this point I am swinging a bag containing two bottles of Laphroaig and have tasted a wee dram or two, but this is the distillery I am most excited about. Because it not only makes my favourite whisky, it also has the best tasting room I have ever visited.

There is no standing at a wooden bar top, elbow to elbow with other people, here. Lagavulin has a cosy sitting room, panelled in white and Granny Smith green, and with four slumpy armchairs arranged around a wood burner. I am brought a dram of the sixteen along with one of the Distillers Edition, a whisky that is double-matured in Pedro Ximénez sherry casks. It is sweet but still spicy, and I settle in to warm up by the fire and slip into daydreams of Scottish touring to come. Naturally, I leave with another bottle or two.

My final stop is at Ardbeg. This is the distillery many find easiest to visit – largely because it has a café. For those who are a little nervous of whisky tasting and saying the right thing, or perhaps worrying that if they don't want to buy a bottle they shouldn't even poke their nose into the shop, this is a welcome excuse to visit. And there's great fish pie to boot.

The café and shop are in the same room and so I check out the merchandise while I wait for my food. It is quiet and the man on the till asks if I'd like any help. I ask what is for sale here that I can't get anywhere else. He smiles. "There isn't much of the Supernova Committee Release from 2015 left," he says. "We'll probably sell out quite soon." This is distillery-speak for a great investment. I look across at the bags I have accumulated and decide there is room for just one more.

The next morning I am supposed to be leaving by ferry from Port Ellen. The wind hasn't let up, though, and it seems that CalMac have already alerted everyone on Islay that the ferry will now leave from Port Askaig before I even get out of bed. On my way into breakfast the woman on reception calls over to me about the change; then I get a text message from CalMac. On my way out a different member of staff tells me once again that I must go to Port Askaig instead of Port Ellen. I am starting to understand just how vital a link to the mainland is for these islanders. The idea of missing the ferry seems to instil real panic in people.

I am also starting to love CalMac even more. When I get to the ferry terminal I am boarded bang on time but some twenty minutes after we were due to leave, my window in the café is still looking down on the cottages of the village. This is, naturally, rather annoying, but just as I am wondering what's going on an announcement comes over the tannoy. CalMac are taxiing everyone who was supposed to be on this ferry but had turned up in Port Ellen across the island. I don't know what the cost of this would have been, but I do know how hard it can be to find a vacant taxi on this island. Finding enough to get everyone to the right ferry port on short notice is truly impressive. I can't help but think that in most places I have travelled – outside of Scotland, that is – those people would have been left stranded.

CHAPTER FIFTEEN

Arran and the Trossachs

By the time I reach Arran I have covered five thousand miles. Scotland is, it is fair to say, not a small country. Google puts its land area at around thirty thousand square miles, and if you were to take off on a flight from Edinburgh, close to the border with England in the south, and fly to Sumburgh on Shetland in the north, you would be in the air for roughly an hour and fifteen minutes. That's almost exactly the same as flying south instead to London. Three months of constant travelling here is still nowhere near enough to see it all. I can't believe I ever thought that Scotland could be easily 'ticked off'.

This is why Arran is so enchanting. If you have just, say, a long weekend to spend in Scotland, make it here. You might think you would miss out on plenty of Scottish classics by doing so. Castles? Brodick Castle stands above the bay you'll most likely enter by ferry. Beaches? Arran has sandy strands on every coast. Whisky? Arran Distillery in Lamlash makes a very fine single malt. It may not be as dramatic an island as Skye, but it isn't as crowded either.

Arran is also where the Highland Boundary Fault reaches

its westernmost extremity. It quite literally cuts the island down the middle, putting half of it in the Lowlands and half in the Highlands. You can spend your morning bounding up Highland hills, eagles circling overhead, and your afternoon romping across rolling countryside to reach a sandy beach.

What's more, Brodick is a proper community. One where you can visit the supermarket, take a yoga class and order a Chinese takeaway. Although I love the Isles I normally conclude with a heavy heart that I simply couldn't live on an island. Arran is different. You can be in Glasgow in under two hours – I can imagine that I could live here.

Arran doesn't wait for you to arrive to start working her charms on you, either. On previous trips I had flown past her beaches bathed in sunshine and desperately wanted to be down there. I had caught sight of her mountains from the coasts of Kintyre and Ayrshire, and now I was staring straight across at her from Skipness, just a few miles from the ferry ports of Kennacraig for Islay, and Claonaig for Arran.

I have stopped at Skipness on the off chance that the seafood cabin will be open this late in the season, and find several tables of diners chomping down crab rolls and grilled queen scallops. A sign pinned to the side of the cabin – essentially a very large wooden shed – tells me that the food is *Freshly prepared by one person*. This is local seafood cooked with love.

I order a hot smoked salmon roll and a plate of langoustines, then take a seat on a bench in the large garden, crossing my fingers that the moody grey sky above my head does not herald rain. To my left is Skipness Castle, partially obscured by a giant tree, its grass fenced off to keep out the sheep and cows that dot the rest of the landscape. To my right is Arran, a soft cloak of mist making her appear like a watercolour painting, milky shafts of autumn sunshine picking out the odd white cottage and giving Kilbrannan Sound a gleam. I can't imagine many better spots for lunch, even in this chilly weather.

Most people's first impression of Arran comes from sailing into the main town of Brodick, crossing from Ardrossan, just under an hour's drive south-west of Glasgow. I am coming from the opposite direction and so will start my tour in Lochranza. This means beginning with the Highlands, and I am not surprised to find that Lochranza is every inch the Highland village, its row of squat white cottages clinging to the lowest slopes of the mustard-and-olive-coloured mountains at their backs. A partially ruined castle stands at the centre of it all, on a promontory that juts out into the glassy loch.

Lochranza is also home to the island's distillery, and I pop in for a wee taste. The distillery is the only one on Arran, and when it produced a three-year-old whisky in 1998 it was the first (legal) dram of Arran whisky for some 160 years. When I tell the shop staff that my favourite whisky from here is the Machrie Moor, a more heavily peated single malt, they smile. "We're building a new distillery in Lagg," they tell me. "It'll focus on more heavily peated whiskies. There's talk of expanding the range." The whisky industry, after all, is booming.

From Lochranza the road passes through Highland Arran to Sannox. It's a drive that takes me only about fifteen minutes but instantly becomes one of my favourites in Scotland, if not the world. On either side of the tarmac, mountains rear up. The first snow of the year has fallen and their tops are brilliant white, as if icing sugar has been dusted over them. The cold turn has brought the wildlife down from the highest peaks and the faintest movement of brown on brown signifies a herd of deer, stalking across the hillside with the sort of swagger that can come only from being the largest, surest species.

As I round a corner the almost perfect pyramid of the island's highest mountain, Goat Fell, practically smacks me in the eye. At almost exactly the same time an eagle very nearly smacks me in the passenger side window, its soaring bulk of feather, beak and claw descending suddenly across the road before a lightning-fast reaction sees it change direction and swoop back upwards. I feel as if the wildlife is in charge here. Compelled to stop, I pull in at the next parking place and take a short stroll along a burn, feeling the mountains around me and watching another herd of deer moving across the hillside.

As if to prove that exploring Arran means coming within near-touching distance of some pretty impressive wildlife, as I drive into the village of Sannox a shadow descends from the top of the windscreen immediately above my head. Naturally distracted, I look up, not for a moment expecting to see a heron happily gliding along above the car, accompanying me as I return to the coast. I reckon that if Arran has a 'big five', I have just seen three of them.

Keen to spend some time in a town, I have chosen to base myself in Brodick, at the gorgeous red sandstone hotel, The Douglas. My room has huge bay windows overlooking the bay and, I am assured when I check in, straight across to Goat Fell. On my arrival, though, thick grey clouds are billowing down the hillside behind Brodick Castle, obscuring all else from view.

It is a different story the next morning, when I open the curtains to see Goat Fell staring back at me, her white slopes picked out in the dusky pink of the day's sunrise. Looking the other way, I watch the CalMac ferry tying up after the day's first sailing from Ardrossan. Once again I am struck by the idea that I could spend a lot of time here, though it may well have to mean moving into the hotel's Goat Fell Suite. I can't imagine there's a room with a better view on the island.

Just outside of Brodick a collection of businesses seem almost to have lined up to prove my point that Arran really does have everything. At Home Farm is Arran Aromatics, a bath, body and home fragrance company whose products I've seen in hotels across Scotland, as well as the Arran Cheese Shop. A few hundred metres up the road is the Cladach Pottery, Arran Graphics and the workshop of Alan MacKenzie, who makes leather bags. Not to mention the Arran Brewery, where I find a selection of beers far wider than I had imagined, from the Arran Blonde I have seen in plenty of pubs to my new favourite, Arran Sunset. Naturally, I stock up for sitting in my bay window later on.

Just behind the brewery the trail up Goat Fell begins. This is the easiest route up to the island's highest point but, not being an experienced winter walker, the walk is not on my list of things to do this time. Instead I have plans to climb a mountain more befitting a lone winter hiker: Dun Fionn. This is a far easier walk than Goat Fell, up to just 172 metres (rather than 874), and it promises views of somewhere I have always wanted to see: Holy Isle. There is also easy parking at Kerr's Port near the village of Lamlash and it is from here that I get my first proper look at Holy Isle, a chunky triangular ridge of an island that dominates the waters off Lamlash.

For now I am turning my back, and heading up a path that remains slightly crusted with ice at this early hour. It is just crispy enough not to be muddy, and by picking the bits knitted together by grass to place my foot I am fairly certain of not sinking boot-deep into the freezing ground. Wet feet on a day like today would be truly miserable.

As I reach the Iron Age hill fort at the top of Dun Fionn, all is peaceful. I watch a kite riding the thermals above the gunmetal-grey waters offshore and mist rising like smoke from the forest. I am aware of how close to the mainland I am here, the ferry almost constantly in view and Ayrshire sitting on the horizon, only sixteen miles or so away across the water. This is far from a remote location, and once again I can imagine how different things would have been when the waterways were the highways. Arran would once have been very much at the centre of things.

Things have, of course, changed dramatically, and Arran is just one more place in Scotland to still be recovering from the Clearances to this day. The island was forever altered by the forced relocation of its people from their homes in the interior, and today all bar one of Arran's villages sit on the coast.

With its population around its shores, Arran's hinterland can seem an empty place. But it is important to remember that this is a man-made wilderness, and that it is far quieter today than it would have been pre Clearances. In some parts of the island I spot tracks that lead to nowhere, the entrances to homes long since abandoned. Landowner the Duke of Hamilton cleared families from smallholdings to create one large sheep farm, forcing some seven hundred people to leave the island. Many went to Canada.

Many of them left from Lamlash, and it is here in the heart of the village that I find something truly unusual: a monument to those who were cleared off their land. To my knowledge there is only one other in Scotland, at Helmsdale in Sutherland, and it is shocking that such an important – and, frankly, devastating – event in Scottish history is only marked officially in a couple of places. The memorial in Lamlash wasn't even erected by the Scottish government; it was paid for by the descendants of those cleared from their Arran homes. It is an understated marker, a set of stones surrounded by a sort of rock garden, its plants growing in neat clumps apart from one hardy climber which has wound its way up one of the stones. It stands here on the waterfront between the two possible outcomes of being cleared from your ancestral lands – the water, from which the *Caledonia* ship departed for New Brunswick in 1829, and the snug row of white cottages that offered new homes for those who would try and make a living on the coast. Today in the sunshine these cottages look appealing, with their green-painted front doors and woodwork, a matching coloured bench sitting outside each one. But there is no getting away from the fact that they are tiny – and that no home that is forced upon you can ever be seen in all that rosy a glow.

Arran's south is bucolic. As I head southwards the mountains retreat entirely from view, the landscape flattening out as the trees become more plentiful. Just past Lamlash I call in at Arran Fine Foods to pick up some of the island's famous mustard and some spicy chutney, and am given two boxes of shortbread for free. "I'll only eat them myself otherwise," says the man on the counter as he loads them into a bag with the jars. Such generosity is rare back in London.

The island's third-largest village is the sprawling Whiting Bay, once home to the longest pier in Scotland. This allowed steamships to dock, bringing visitors to the south of the island by a much more direct route than is possible now. It was closed in the early 1960s and today only a tiny jetty remains of it. The village itself is silent aside from the birds – oystercatchers calling from the beach – and the local primary school at playtime.

There is still reason to stop in Whiting Bay, for its pleasant sandy beach as well as for the wonderful Bay Stores, a funky mini supermarket that is better stocked than my local Waitrose with fresh meats and local cheeses aplenty. It also has proper coffees, served at tiny tables gathered near the window. I order mine to take away and sit on a bench overlooking the beach, watching the tide slipping out and exposing the seaweed. It occurs to me that everywhere I have felt like sitting on Arran I have found a bench, often several. This is an island that seems to be constantly tempting you to stay awhile.

I want to make a loop of the island, and so I am heading onwards south, to Kildonan and the beach many locals have told me is the island's best. This seems in large part to be due to the view, of Ailsa Craig in the waters offshore. Few islands are as dramatic as this one, a perfect volcanic mound that sits on the horizon like a floating pyramid of stone some 340 metres high.

The beach is more than just the view, though, and I spend a happy half-hour poking around on the rocks and taking sun-soaked pictures. Ailsa Craig appears tiny from this far away (some thirteen miles), but the island of Pladda sits just offshore, its lighthouse gleaming white in the sunlight. If I forget that I am wearing two coats today I could pretend that it was summer.

It is a different story at Machrie Moor, my final stop on Arran. The car park here is deserted and the rain has started up once more, dumping great droplets of water onto the already boggy landscape.

This is the sort of place that makes me dizzy with the effort of attempting to even begin to comprehend the passage of time. I read on the signs here that this land was altered by climate change in around 700 BC, turning it from fertile farmland into peat bog. The earliest sign of human activity is from about 3500 BC, and the first stone circles here are thought to have been erected around 2000 BC.

But it is this sentence that really makes my head spin: *Most of our knowledge of [the stone circles] comes from scientific excavations carried out in the 1980s.* That nobody knew anything much about this place for the several thousand years in between Machrie Moor being a sacred landscape and home to a community, and us modern-day tourists standing here on a muddy moor looking at pictures of ploughs and urns, is staggering. For all of that time people must have just shrugged their shoulders at the stones as they went about their business, or perhaps ignored them entirely. I feel very lucky to be here in the brief blink of time that is the post-1980s, when we are far enough along earth's ever-moving timeline to be able to read about what this landscape may have been. When we can be certain of a few things, at least.

I am sorry to be leaving Arran, but, glancing at the back seat of my car as I board the ferry bound for Ardrossan, I seem to be taking rather a lot of her with me. A bottle of whisky, a selection of beers, a bagload of cheese, some mustard, a jar of chutney, that gifted shortbread – Arran hasn't so much got under my skin as into my stomach.

I have plans to be in Glasgow in a few days' time and so I am making only a whistle-stop tour of Loch Lomond and the Trossachs. This is Scotland's other national park. It was designated first (before the Cairngorms) and has a long history of welcoming day trippers and holidaymakers. One of its downsides, in fact, is that it can attract rather too many visitors, and after weeks of travelling in farther-flung parts of the country, this is where I see Scotland's tourism infrastructure kick back into full swing. There is so much more traffic here, and so many more signs for boat trips and other excursions.

Loch Lomond is the largest loch (or lake) in Britain. It has thirty islands scattered across it and more varieties of fish are found here than in any other Scottish loch. It is a marvellous place for a few days by the water, and on a previous trip I had stayed at Cameron House hotel and taken a seaplane flight above the loch.

It lends itself perfectly to this, its calm, tranquil surface the ideal runway, and I loved my window seat for the 'discovery' tour. We flew above the loch for a bird's-eye view of the islands before heading northwards to fly past Ben Lomond, Scotland's most southerly Munro, and on to the Arrochar Alps. The Highland Boundary Fault runs across Loch Lomond, and these hills are the start of the Highlands. Everything north of here seemed to rear up ahead of us, while looking to my left I could see down along the shores of Loch Long and out into the Firth of Clyde. The landscape laid out beneath me had only made me want to explore more of this beautiful country.

On this trip I have certainly done just that, and now I am heading for the Trossachs, a region I had mostly skipped over in the past. Although it is close to both Glasgow and Stirling, it isn't exactly on the way to anywhere and is a rather undefined area. In the past, my guidebook tells me, the name 'the Trossachs' – which roughly translates as 'crossing place' – was only used to refer to the wooded glen between Loch Katrine and Loch Achray. And so I have decided that with limited time I will head straight here, to climb Ben A'an, which stands above Loch Katrine at a height of 340 metres.

Ben A'an is another mountain that is such a perfect pyramid

that it resembles a Toblerone segment. It stands in a rounded-off conical peak looking down on the trail that leads up it and, I am told at my hotel, promises one of the best effort-to-reward ratios of any hill in Scotland.

This, along with the day's fine weather, means that there are several families making their way up Ben A'an today. I find myself catching up with small groups occasionally, parents pulling children who must be as young as six or seven out of my way as I pass and say hello. Most of the children look delighted to be climbing a hill and this makes for a pleasant community feel to the walk – there are lots of smiling faces. Even better, the path is a well-made one, and, despite an initial ascent that is so steep it has me stopping to stretch out my calf muscles halfway up, it's an easy climb. I let my mind wander as I pass ferns turned golden by the season and trees now long denuded of their leaves. It is unmistakably autumn.

At the summit I find that the woman at my hotel was right. For fairly little effort I am now looking at one of the most enchanting views in Scotland. A few metres from my feet is a triangular rock that seems to be the highest point of the hill, as if the whole thing really were an entirely straight-sided pyramid. I clamber along the sharp, rocky ridge and find that I can see almost the full length of Loch Katrine. In every direction, all is green and gold and brown. Hills and mountains stretch off to dramatic horizons all around me and the only man-made thing in sight is, well, man. A family with kids in red fleeces clambers up behind me and a boy who must be about ten shouts backwards, "Mum, it's beautiful up here!" I smile in gleeful agreement.

CHAPTER SIXTEEN

Glasgow

Glasgow gets more than its fair share of rain. Despite visiting the city dozens of times, I can only recall one or two occasions when I could have gone an entire day without the need for an umbrella, or at least a decent hood. But, my goodness, it's a welcoming place, the sort of city where it takes five times as long to buy a basket of groceries or check in to a hotel due to the amount of chat that warmly envelops every interaction with a fellow human being. A well-worn cliché this may be, but Glasgow frequently tops lists of the UK's friendliest cities and was voted the friendliest city in the world by a Rough Guides poll in 2016.

That famously chatty Glasgow cliché reared its rather lovely, life-affirming head as soon as I parked up in the car park closest to my hotel. On entering the lift I was aware of a man a few seconds behind me. As the doors began to close I pushed the button to stop them so that he could catch the same elevator as me. We settled into the traditional 'standing staring aimlessly into space' pose I would expect any two strangers in a lift in any city in the world to adopt. But this is Glasgow. "I should walk, really, but

I've been at work," he said, launching into an explanation of his tiredness versus laziness and sparking an animated conversation.

Ultimately, of course, we discussed the weather. "Cracking day," I said.

"Aye, but how long will it last?" he retorted with a smile. Had I said I was only visiting, I bet he would have apologised for the weather.

I decided to enjoy the unexpectedly sunny day with a stroll around the city centre. Despite being several miles up the Clyde River from the Atlantic, Glasgow has always felt like a seaside city to me, and walking along her handsome streets I find that the sound of gulls is creating quite a cacophony. I wander past creamy sandstone buildings flanked by neoclassical columns, their elegant windows glinting in the afternoon light, imagining that at any moment I might find myself faced with the ocean.

Instead I end up in George Square. It is here that Glasgow's reign as second city of the British Empire is perhaps the most apparent, its grand Victorian architecture proudly proclaiming that this is a city of stature. An eighty-foot column stands at its centre, topped by a statue of someone I haven't seen for a while: the great Sir Walter Scott.

A far more interesting statue is found just around the corner, on Royal Exchange Square. It is of Arthur Wellesley, the first Duke of Wellington, but he would perhaps not be all that impressed at the fact that nobody really cares a jot who he is – they care only about his headgear.

This is because his head is almost permanently topped by a traffic cone. Nobody knows exactly how this started (well, actually, *somebody* certainly does), but it has been a tradition since sometime in the 1980s when presumably at least one countercultural revolutionary got absolutely blootered, swiped a traffic cone and clambered up the statue to jam it onto the duke's head.

What has always surprised me is that the council continuously spend time and money removing the cone. They reckon it costs

£100 every time they do this, and every single time they do the cone simply reappears a few days later. The cone even featured in the opening ceremony of the 2014 Commonwealth Games, and when the council tried to make plans to renovate the statue to make it higher there were protests and, naturally, a Facebook group to save the cone. The protestors won and the statue remains the same.

I have always wondered why, if the council's concern is that somebody will either hurt themselves or damage the Grade A listed statue, they don't just leave a cone securely bolted up there and let everyone assume it's an ever-changing one that they keep removing. I also don't understand why some people think the cone gives a depressing image of Glasgow. To me, it has always been a reason to raise a smile, a small practical joke that nods to the city's famously dry sense of humour.

Like many cities in the UK, Glasgow has seen much recent regeneration of its riverside, and on this visit I started by calling in at the shiny new Clydeside Distillery. This stands, you won't be surprised to learn, on the side of the Clyde, on land that was once part of the vast Queen's Dock, named after Queen Victoria and opened in 1877.

The distillery is housed in what was once a pump house and, in typically twenty-first-century style, its architecture retains the bones of that building and adds floor-to-ceiling glass windows for panoramic views along the river. The two copper stills here stand proudly above the water, framed by those windows, heralding the continued presence of craftsmanship on the Clyde and tempting me to sample the new-make spirit that will a few years from now be bottled as a whisky.

Afterwards I head out onto the banks of the Clyde and find myself dwarfed by the Finnieston Crane. This fifty-three-metre-tall cantilevered crane that once lifted railway engines and tanks onto cargo ships for export around the world is a reminder to modern eyes of how busily industrial this area would once have been. It is, after all, just one of the dozens of massive cranes that once stood along the river's banks.

After the Acts of Union in 1707, Scotland gained access to all of England's markets and Glasgow was well placed on the west coast to became a hub of international trade, especially with the Americas. When travelling west from Glasgow, ships had a two- to three-week head start over those leaving from other British and European ports.

The city had a problem, though: the upper stretches of the Clyde were naturally very shallow, the water often only just over a metre or so deep even at high tide at Broomielaw in the city centre. And so, a deep-water port was built at Port Glasgow further downriver. This was a roaring success and by the late eighteenth century more than half of Britain's tobacco was being landed on the Clyde. Some people in the city began to get very rich indeed.

The great businessmen and councillors of the city saw the shimmer of opportunity – and pounds signs, presumably – in the Clyde, and throughout the eighteenth and nineteenth centuries the most eminent engineers of the day set about schemes for dredging the river. The depth of the water was steadily increased and had risen by several metres by the mid nineteenth century. This enabled the city's most famous industry to develop. It was of, course, shipbuilding.

Probably the most famous ship to have been built on the Clyde is the *Cutty Sark*, completed by William Denny and Brothers, downriver at Dumbarton. This is where the River Leven meets the Clyde, and there's evidence to suggest there was shipbuilding on the Leven as early as the fifteenth century.

It was the Dennys, though, who really put Dumbarton on the map, and the shipyard took over the contract for the *Cutty Sark* when rival firm Scott and Linton ran out of cash to finish her. Being British, she was designed to speed tea back from China as quickly as possible, and throughout the 1870s she became known as the fastest ship of the day. In 1874 she sailed from Sydney to London in an unrivalled seventy-three days.

The Clyde's pedigree as the birthing ground of the greatest ships of the nineteenth century and early decades of the twentieth can be seen in the names of the vessels produced by just one of its shipyards, John Brown and Company of Clydebank: RMS *Lusitania*, RMS *Queen Mary*, RMS *Queen Elizabeth*, the *Royal Yacht Britannia*, the *QE2*. At one time in the early 1900s it's estimated that a fifth of the world's ships were built on the Clyde. Throughout the nineteenth and twentieth centuries some thirty thousand ships were built here and the industry employed tens of thousands of people. It is hardly a surprise that when the industry collapsed, Glasgow fell into a period of deep decline.

But today the area around the Clyde is far from dead. As well as the shiny new Clydeside Distillery, also on the site of the old Queen's Dock is the SSE Hydro arena and the SEC Centre, Scotland's largest exhibition centre. BBC Scotland are based across the water, and the overlapping silver shells of the Foster + Partners-designed SEC auditorium, predictably nicknamed the Armadillo, can often be seen in the background of their broadcasts. There is plenty going on here.

There is also plenty going on just up the road in Finnieston, once an industrial service centre of warehouses and docks, today the sort of place that graces national newspapers' lists of the hippest places to live. Every time in the past few years that I've visited 'the strip' of Argyll Street, I've found a trendy new restaurant, café or bar, but it is one of the early adopters that I love the most, a place that has been here since 2009 and seen the cool quota rise all around it.

Crabshakk is teeny, with only a cluster of tables on the mezzanine and a row of them downstairs, plus a few stools at the bar. The fish of the day here is chalked up on – what else? – a blackboard slate. This is brought over when you sit down, and the menu has all the Scottish shellfish classics, from oysters and scallops to mussels and lobster. I've spent many a happy afternoon chomping my way through the *fruits de mer* platter here, and I head straight to the restaurant from the distillery. Within minutes a groaning iced metal dish packed with clams, oysters and langoustines and crowned with crab claws and a lobster shell lands on my table. I do not leave for a very long time indeed.

I have timed my visit to Glasgow to coincide with a football match – the national team are playing a World Cup qualifier against Slovakia. This will be at Hampden Park, the world's oldest international football ground. It was built in 1903 and was the world's largest football stadium until 1950. Though attendance figures fluctuate – and include many thousands of cheeky, gate-jumping fans – Hampden certainly had a higher official capacity than Wembley in London. Glasgow can beat London at many things and passion for football is inarguably one of them.

I also doubt there is anywhere livelier or more fun than Glasgow to watch an international football match. At least, that is, if you're not utterly convinced that the home side cannot possibly win. Scotland unfortunately have a rather poor recent footballing record, and no Scot I have met ever seems to expect them to win anything. Being English, I can see through the Scottish crisis of confidence to a team that have been playing well and can certainly beat Slovakia, their opponents today.

I have plans to join the Tartan Army in The Shed for the vaguely official pre-Hampden party and arrive wearing blue, hoping to blend in. I certainly do that, but I needn't have worried about any anti-English sentiment. The bulk of the army are swinging around the dance floor in the middle of the place, line-dancing with their arms around each other and throwing their hands up in the air to S Club 7's 'Reach for the Stars'. I sip my beer up on the balcony and watch kids with painted faces waving the Saltire above the crowd as 'Flower of Scotland' is belted out by several hundred excited football fans. This is about as far from a hostile environment as I can imagine – and absolutely nobody comments on my accent.

The walk to the ground is a route march along Battlefield Road, all kilts and dark blue Scotland shirts. There is, of course, more singing, and plenty of opportunity to buy scarves, hats and flags along the roadside. I pick up a scarf and enter the ground in search of the ticket-pickup windows.

Despite the queue I cannot help but smile. There are three windows, divided up by surname. Mine falls under N–Z, another window is for A–L, and the third solely for M, Mac and Mc. Only in Scotland would a third of the crowd have surnames starting with just one letter of the alphabet. Clan history is alive and well in Glasgow.

The match itself is a nail-biter. Shots rain down on the goal from both sides and some excellent saves from Slovakian goalkeeper Martin Dúbravka keep the crowd around me in near-silence. I am in a pack of anxious men, shifting from foot to foot in really quite visible pain. Almost every set of arms is seriously folded, heads are down, eyes are all focused straight ahead. There is a sense that it could all go wrong at any moment, and then, finally, it does – for Slovakia.

Scotland have to win this clash to retain any chance of qualifying for the World Cup, and in the eighty-ninth minute a brilliant run down the right wing by Scotland ends with Slovakian defender Martin Škrtel getting to Ikechi Anya's cross only in time to accidentally push the ball over his own line. That it is an own goal doesn't convey how much Scotland deserved their lead, and there is utter jubilation in the stands. I am hugged by people I hadn't previously spoken to, and finally there is singing once again. It is fair to say I am a little drunk on the beer and on the excitement of it all, but I have never been more in love with Scotland's largest city. I feel like I belong.

CHAPTER SEVENTEEN

Stirling and the Central Belt

The following day I am at a border once again. Not one between countries this time, but one that is an ancient fault line, one that has been the frontier for longer than anybody can remember.

This is Stirling, the centuries-old crossing point between Highland and Lowland. A place that marked the beginning of the Highlands before anybody knew anything at all about the Highland Boundary Fault. Here stands the Auld Brig, or Stirling Old Bridge, vaulting across the Forth at the easiest crossing point for many miles. The medieval arched stone bridge that still stands here has been crossed by every monarch from James I to Charles I, and was the subject of many a battle over centuries. He who controlled the bridge controlled the country. This has long been Scotland's crossroads.

For me today it holds a similar role. This is my crossroads, the point at which I will turn south and begin to head for home. I feel prepared and entirely unprepared for the end of my journey.

With many miles to cover in my final weekend on the road, I have decided to cram all of Stirling's attractions into just one day. And so I find myself breaking a sweat on the hike uphill to the Wallace Monument.

The path here circles upwards through the woodland towards a Victorian Gothic stone tower that stands in testimony to the man who is surely the most famous knight in Scottish history, William Wallace. A sign tells me that this is a memorial to *Scotland's first national hero*, and various wood carvings line the route. One is a mini version of the monument, another shows local aviators the Barnwell brothers, another is a train large enough for kids to sit on. I am baffled by their links to Wallace until I realise: Wallace's legacy is to this day a belief that Scotland can do it. Whatever 'it' might be.

On the second floor of the monument itself I find the Hall of Heroes. This collection of busts of inspiring great Scots features plenty of names you would expect – Robert the Bruce, Robert Burns, James Watt – and celebrates the legacy of Wallace. His victories over the English during the First War of Scottish Independence brought pride to the hearts of many Scots. It is a pride that is all too often missing from Scotland's historic attractions, and it is refreshing that in this room Scotland is far from the underdog.

Continuing up among the masonry I find myself stepping out onto a terrace at the monument's top. This is called the Crown, and it has one hell of a view. From up here Stirling's position at the crossroads of Scotland is clear. To the south, jade-green fields roll off to a distant horizon; to the north, great lumpen hills sparse with trees stand between me and anything further. The natural barrier they would have been to a journey north is obvious, as is the fact that control of the crossing point here was a very enticing prize indeed.

It is no surprise, then, that so many battles have been fought in this area, and that my next destination – and the reason for my hurry – is Bannockburn. The National Trust for Scotland have taken a very different approach here to the sombre tone of Culloden, and an interactive battle experience is the main draw. This means timed slots and tickets that cannot be changed, and so I find myself here in plenty of time, for fear of missing one of Scotland's absolutely unmissable sites.

This gives me plenty of time to wander out to the statue of the big man himself, Robert the Bruce. Bruce came along after Wallace had been captured by the English and viciously hung, drawn and quartered. He was crowned King of Scotland in 1603 and set about taking the country back by force. He had much success for many years, success which culminated in the Battle of Bannockburn in 1314 – perhaps Scotland's most significant defeat of the English.

At this site there are no marked war graves. All there is to see outside is the monument of Bruce, wielding an axe atop his warhorse in full chain mail, and the memorial cairn for those who died here – or, by all best guesses, near here – standing in the centre of a rotunda complete with fluttering Saltire.

If this were all there was to see at Bannockburn I doubt it would attract quite the number of visitors I find standing around inside the inevitable gift shop. Most of the other visitors are families and there are plenty of excited children, desperate to find out if their role in the interactive battle will be to fight for the English or the Scots. Everyone, I suspect, would like to fight for the Scots, but since they were grossly outnumbered by the English on that fateful day, few will get to stand beneath the Saltire once we get to the game itself.

This is an educational experience above all and so first we must be trained. We are taken into a room full of screens that tell the stories of the people, both knights and commoners, who fought for king and country. These are interactive, and standing listening to a cut-out person speaking about their role in the battle is a little like meeting a hologram. Around me everyone is engrossed in the stories from both sides and, as we have been told to learn about battle tactics to help us in the battle to come, there is rapt attention from even the youngest children.

Before there is time to really take it all in we are called through into the battle room by the battle master. A small doorway leads through into a circular room lined with screens; a console stands in the centre surrounded by stools. Each stool has a number and we are sent to these more or less at random, with siblings deliberately sent to opposite sides of the room. Soon it dawns on us that the seats furthest to the right are the Scottish knights – and that there are far fewer of them than there are of those of us cast as English. They are outnumbered two or perhaps even three to one.

The game begins with each of us tasked with deciding to attack, move or stay put, and on the first run around the circle not a single person chooses to attack. About a quarter of the time people choose to run for the hills, literally, and the battle master has to tell us off for not getting stuck in and fighting.

As the English, we are trying to capture Bruce, but the last woman to make a play on behalf of our side flaps her hands and says she "feel[s] bad for the king". She decides she will retreat and we are all far too polite to tell her she has been ridiculous. Fortunately at this point the game itself takes over and the moves we have already made play out on screen in front of us. Despite our cowardly tactics, the English, with our superior numbers, win the battle. Scotland, our guide tells us, hardly ever win. Which of course only makes Bruce's successful battle command all the more impressive.

Nobody visits Stirling for, well, Stirling. An attractive city it may be, but its big-hitter attractions – its castle, the Wallace Monument and Bannockburn – are why any of us are really here, and there are few reasons to spend much time in the city centre itself.

The best reason to allow time for a stop here is the Engine Shed. This is a centre for understanding Scotland's 'built heritage'.

Or, to put it another way, the things that human beings have done to the landscape. It had only recently opened on my visit and I had heard that it was an excellent place to gain an overview of the country. It's a shame I'm visiting on one of my final days in Scotland.

I park in a large car park on Forthside Way and find myself surrounded by the sort of built environment nobody has a whole lot of love for: those restaurants like Frankie & Benny's and Beefeater that only seem to pop up near cinemas and in retail parks. The walk to the shed isn't exactly inspiring and I don't feel too sad not to have booked a hotel in the city centre.

The Engine Shed itself more than makes up for its unexciting surroundings. This was once a goods transfer shed set between the railway and the River Forth. Nobody knows exactly when it was built but we do know that it was around the turn of the twentieth century, and that the shed saw military use. The details of its construction were subject to an information blackout.

Today it's a glorious, light open space with a vast map of Scotland mounted on wheels at its centre. Historic Environment Scotland run the shed as a hub of building and restoration advice for those looking after historic buildings, and there are plenty of courses you can take here. The main attraction for visitors, though, is that map, which comes to life when you have an iPad in your hands. These are issued at the front desk free of charge and immediately I am poking around, gaining access to more information on everything from the Forth Bridge to the geology of the Isles using augmented reality. I haven't seen this technology used in an attraction like this before and it is sheer genius – much like the experience at Bannockburn, it makes learning about Scotland feel like playing a game. I trace the lines of my travels with a finger and find plenty I have missed along the way.

The peril of a trip that is a defined period of time – a weekend break, say, or a month-long research trip – is that what you can squeeze into your itinerary is finite. I know that I have crammed in a lot but still there are places I find myself zooming in on with sadness. Why didn't I see that Iron Age broch on the west coast, that crumbling castle on the east? And still the Northern Isles sit there taunting me, the largest piece of the puzzle that I have had to leave out of this trip. I try to keep from kicking myself by dreaming of my next adventure in this endlessly bewitching country.

One final place in Stirling demands to be seen, though, and so I hand back my iPad and make my way up through the city centre to the only castle that can truly rival Edinburgh when it comes to imposing locations.

Stirling Castle stands atop a volcanic crag that has been fortified since the Iron Age. Sheer cliffs plunge some 75 metres on three sides, and from up here I can see for miles around, including, of course, a fine view of the Auld Brig. It would have been impossible for anyone seeking to claim Scotland's crossroads to sneak up unannounced.

During the Wars of Independence, Stirling Castle was under siege constantly, changing hands eight times in forty-six years. The Battles of Stirling Bridge and Bannockburn placed it back in Scottish hands, but the English were tenacious and it wasn't until 1342 that the castle returned more permanently to Scottish control.

All that bloody conflict is hard to imagine on a sunny day atop this ancient volcano, though. From the ramparts, I find myself looking out over a garden blooming with yellow roses and purple heathers, towards the rounded, grassy remains of what was once a formal garden in the fields far below. Birds land in the trees around me, and I find myself squinting into the warm late-autumn sun.

It is easy to forget that the imposing castles we visit today were in fact homes. They were not austere stone fortresses built only to repel invaders; they were warm family houses with roaring fires and brightly painted woodwork, tapestries and paintings. Stirling Castle was perhaps the most important home in Scotland, that of the Stuarts, and the birthplace of their most famous daughter, Mary, Queen of Scots.

Mary Stuart was the heir to her father James V's throne when he died in 1542. That she was only six days old when he died is not the saddest thing that ever befell her. She lost two husbands: one (the French king, Francis II) to an ear infection when she was aged just eighteen; the other to suspected murder by her, ahem, third husband. Abdication was then forced upon her in 1567 and she sought refuge in England with her first cousin once removed, Queen Elizabeth I.

Unfortunately, Mary had a legitimate claim to the English throne and, being Catholic to Elizabeth's Protestant, was the favoured monarch of many powerful people. Plots to murder Elizabeth and install Mary as queen instead were rife and so Elizabeth had Mary beheaded in 1587, suspecting her of plotting to murder her. You can see, frankly, where she may have got her suspicions.

Mary's son, James VI, fared better, becoming King of Scotland on Mary's forced abdication and King of England in 1603 when Elizabeth herself died with no heir. This was the Union of the Crowns – which persists to this day – and it caused James to turn his back on Scotland. The castle benefited, though, when news of his one and only return visit in 1616 led to more than £13,000 being spent on repairing the royal residences. This would be about £2 million today – quite the bill for a flying visit.

Today the Royal Palace has been refurbished to look as it might have done around the 1540s and the medieval hall still stands much as it did when it was built in 1503. It was – and remains – the largest and finest medieval hall in Scotland, and is spacious enough for five hundred people to meet for a state banquet. It is also large enough, in my personal experience, for Visit Scotland to host a lively ceilidh and whisky tasting that I only remember the first half of.

My favourite story from the castle isn't of formal, regal life. It is of the so-called 'Bird Man of Stirling', an Italian alchemist called John Damian who promised James IV that he could turn base metals into gold. Naturally, this turned out to be nonsense, but was undoubtedly not nearly as entertaining as his claim to be able to fly to France dressed in a chicken suit. In 1507 Damian built wings and glued feathers onto them before gathering the king and his court on the castle's battlements. He then leapt off, flapped frantically – and ended up in a dunghill, breaking his leg in the process. He is said to have blamed the "wrong kind of feathers". In a later life he would surely have worked for British Rail.

One of Scotland's most surprising attractions lies just south of Stirling, a couple of miles from the town of Falkirk. Now, it may be true that Falkirk doesn't exactly top many a Scottish holiday itinerary, but if you have any interest in engineering whatsoever, let me say this: you simply must visit the Falkirk Wheel.

This space-age-looking marvel of engineering is the world's first and only rotating boat lift. It joins the Forth and Clyde Canal to the Union Canal and takes about four minutes to bridge the waters of the two. This is rather quicker than the full day the staircase of eleven locks that previously stood here used to take. It opened in 2002 and stands thirty-five metres tall. It can lift 300 tonnes of water in under five minutes using – and here's the staggering thing – only the amount of electricity it would take to boil eight household kettles.

On seeing the wheel I am blown away. It is so much larger than I had imagined, standing in a circular canal pound just off the lower Forth and Clyde Canal. High above me the Union Canal comes to an abrupt end on the hillside, carried across to the top of the wheel by a high suspended waterway that looks like the track of a futuristic monorail. It reminds me of the one at Disneyland.

The wheel itself is shaped more like two end-to-end apostrophes, cast in solid metal. The head of each one holds a gondola and it is these that hold the narrowboats, rotating at a slow and steady speed to bring the upper one down to the Forth and Clyde while the lower sweeps up to the Union.

Scottish Canals clearly understand that nobody can see the wheel without wanting to take a ride on it, and there are tours throughout the day. A group of us board the boat that will take us on a joyride up to the Union Canal, a short way along it and then back down on the wheel, and our guide begins talking about how the system works as the gondola is shut off from the canal and released for its ascent. There is much talk of hydraulics, axels and gears, but just like I was in my school science lessons, I am distracted by the view.

We are slowly rising up above the landscape of Scotland's Central Belt. This has long been the country's centre of population, running from Glasgow in the west to Edinburgh in the east, and it remains home to the majority of its people.

Although I can see the usual patchwork of hills and fields, there is also still plenty of industry in evidence and our guide points out the Grangemouth Refinery and the Port of Grangemouth, Scotland's largest container port. He also points towards the River Carron, where once the great Carron Ironworks stood. This was opened in 1759 to exploit the coalfields of nearby Kinnaird and was for a time the greatest iron foundry in the world. In 1770 James Watt made his steam engine here, and from 1779 Carron produced thousands of cannonades for Nelson's Royal Navy. Shrapnel shells were developed here from 1784, and over the years the place turned out everything from manhole covers to Britain's iconic red telephone boxes. I ask the guide if there is anything to see of it now. "Aye, you can still see the clock tower," he says, "but that's all that's left of it now."

We pootle gently along the canal for a couple of hundred metres or so, cruising through a dripping stone tunnel and passing waving grasses along the banks, close enough that we could reach out and touch them, were a window not in the way. It is a beautifully pastoral landscape, and one that reminds me of my childhood home in Wiltshire once again.

Although my trip is almost over, I do have one more stop to make before turning south towards the border once again. I am off to see two larger-than-life mythical beasts – *The Kelpies*. They stand at the eastern entrance to the Forth and Clyde Canal just a few miles from the wheel.

This part of the canal was built as an extension in 2013, to link the canal to the River Forth and make it easier to travel by water from the east of Scotland to the west, or vice versa. This is a project that would certainly have gained far less interest – and press coverage – without the installation of the world's largest equine sculpture, and it is the two silver horses' heads that have brought me here to gawp.

Because they really are extraordinary. Made up of 928 stainless-steel skin plates, they glint in the sunlight and catch the eye for miles around. They are thirty metres high and weigh three hundred tonnes apiece. And they are attracting as much of a crowd as the wheel, and even more selfie-taking. Myself included, naturally.

Kelpies are mythical animals said to have the strength and endurance of ten horses, and so they were chosen by Scottish Canals to represent the amazing animals who kept the waterways moving: the horses who pulled barges, wagons, ploughs and coal ships across Scotland. I am reminded of pictures I saw as a child, of my local canal lined with horses, and turn to remark on this memory to anyone who might listen. I realise with a jolt that I am getting lonely – and that I am ready to go home.

From *The Kelpies* I am heading south and my final few days on the road are to be spent in the far south-west of Scotland, a region that is all too often forgotten. Scotland's border with England is a diagonal line – from Berwick in the east, where I started this trip, south-west to Gretna Green – and so there is a whole lot more of Scotland to the south of Glasgow than there is to the south of Edinburgh.

I haven't, frankly, left nearly enough time to do it justice. Just a few nights of my trip remain and I still have a huge chunk of Scotland that I hope to see. I decide that I must stick to the highlights and so I head first to Alloway, the birthplace of the man who could be said to be the most famous Scot ever to walk this earth. Not to mention one of the most talented writers the world has ever seen.

I am talking, of course, about Robert Burns, Scotland's national bard and the reason so many people down south spend one night every January eating haggis and drinking whisky. Burns was born on the 25th January 1759 in Alloway on the coast of Ayrshire, more or less right opposite the southern end of Arran. And so, on a sunny day's drive south along the Firth of Clyde, the mountains of Arran and the volcanic lump of Ailsa Craig are once again stealing the show. I find I am missing the Isles already.

Robert Burns' birthplace is a significant site, with not only the tiny three-room cottage he was born in to see, but also a memorial garden, the fifteenth-century bridge Brig o' Doon, and the world's leading museum on the subject of Burns. It would be easy to spend at least half a day here discovering more about Burns – something I realised I very much needed to do.

Because I have to admit that until the very moment I stepped inside the museum I couldn't have told you anything much about Scotland's bard aside from the fact that he had written the words for 'Auld Lang Syne'. Growing up in England I had studied William Shakespeare endlessly at school, dissecting his sonnets and performing his plays, and yet I do not recall Burns ever once being so much as mentioned. This seems to me an unforgivable oversight in a supposedly British education.

And so I lapped up knowledge in the museum. I discovered that 'Auld Lang Syne' has been sung in more Hollywood movies than any other song besides 'Happy Birthday', and that Burns is said to have written a whopping nine hundred works: 340 songs and 560 poems. This despite him living to only thirty-seven.

In the Victorian era Burns was greatly admired and people sought out any souvenir they could of the great man. He is said to have inspired the work of J. D. Salinger, Maya Angelou, Seamus Heaney, Michael Jackson and Tracey Emin among many others. Few writers can have had such a long-lasting legacy in the creative arts and yet in England, Burns is still too often dismissed, his works said to be difficult to understand.

This is partly because Burns chose to write in his native tongue, Scots. Burns championed the continued use of Scots throughout his life. It was his mother tongue and it is fitting that the museum is presented in Scots.

Fitting and very educational, it turns out. Take this sentence, for example: *He yaised vieve descriptions o nature tae gie a heeze tae the emotional impact o a poem or sang.* I don't believe that anybody could read that and maintain that Scots isn't a separate language from English. With a few translations underneath I was able to understand that it was saying that he used vivid descriptions of nature to give weight to the emotional impact of a poem or song. Few places I have visited get to the heart of how English and Scots are two distinct but related languages in the way this museum does. I feel like maybe I should be learning Scots the way I am learning Spanish.

From the museum it is a short walk through pleasant woodland to Burns' birthplace itself, where I find that the National Trust have jazzed up the cottage with some rather odd audiovisual effects and props. Personally I would have preferred to tour the cottage without the animal noises and fake fire crackle but it is interesting to see how a farmer's family would have lived and to marvel at the way Robert pulled himself out of poverty and into high society.

That Burns only lived to the age of thirty-seven is a great loss for Scotland. He was a radical, against monarchy and slavery when so many others weren't, and a champion of the rights of the little guy. He had the ear of plenty of powerful people and, had he lived longer, would surely have written many more great works. It is ironic, too, that he is thought to have died of endocarditis, an infection in the heart that would now be treated using penicillin. Penicillin was of course discovered by Alexander Fleming, another Ayrshire farmer's son. Once again I am struck by how much Scotland has given to the world, and by how much more loudly the country should be shouting about its achievements.

After Ayrshire I had plans to spend the night on the so-called Scottish Riviera at Kirkcudbright – a place pronounced in no way phonetically (it is said: 'Ker-coo-bry'). The town sits in Dumfries and Galloway, the region said to be the warmest part of Scotland, which makes sense since it is the furthest south. It is also perhaps the most reminiscent of England, and as I drive through its heartland I find I am passing rolling hills and farmland that echo Wiltshire once again. Dense woodland leads down to tranquil lochs and I am once again slowed to tractor pace as farm vehicles pull out in front of me.

But Kirkcudbright is well worth the wait and on a sunny morning here the pastel houses, toothy, ruined castle and glass-like harbour make it obvious why this town has a reputation for being an artists' bolthole. It is quite simply lovely.

With its numerous galleries and a lively fishing port, Kirkcudbright would make for an excellent weekend break or the ideal place to stay and write a book. Sadly, though, I am heading once again for the border, and for one final night in Scotland, at Gretna Green.

First, I have a couple of things that I want to see. I have long been keen to visit Sweetheart Abbey and so, turning south from the town of Dumfries, I find myself delving through the countryside once again, weaving around farmers' fields and clumps of woodland on narrow roads lined with hedgerows.

The abbey itself was founded by Lady Dervorguilla as a

tribute to her beloved husband John Balliol. And it is here that it all gets a little bit weird. Because when Balliol died in 1268 Lady Dervorguilla had his heart embalmed. And then she carried it around with her – everywhere she went, it is said – until her own death in 1289. That's more than twenty years of dragging a preserved piece of human flesh around and seems just a little, well, excessive. She even called it her "sweet, silent companion".

This story means that the abbey is more well known than it might otherwise have been. It's a stunner too, all towering red sandstone arches. There is quite a lot of it still standing and I am able to stand at one end of the nave and feel its grandeur. Fluted columns march along on either side to reach a gabled wall still holding the rose-shaped stonework that would once have been filled by stained glass.

It is possible to see where Lady Dervorguilla and her husband are buried; her, naturally, clutching his heart to her bosom. I also discover that Edward I is said to have spent Christmas 1300 here, saying, "If this is Scotland, I want more of it." Sadly, he meant that he wanted to take it for England, not enjoy it as I am today. But his words hold an echo for me on my final day in Scotland. I also want more of it.

One thing I certainly want to do is visit the Devil's Porridge Museum, because how could anybody fail to be intrigued by a museum with that for a name? Just seven miles from the border with England and just to the west of Gretna Green, this modern museum tells the story of the munitions factory that was once Britain's greatest. It could be said, in fact, that this is the place that won the First World War.

On some days during the war the British Army could fire a million shells. That's an awful lot of ammunition needing to be produced back on home soil, and it led to a crisis. Britain simply wasn't producing enough and the Allies were losing the war. So during 1915, Minister for Munitions (and later Prime Minister)

David Lloyd George ordered the creation of more than a hundred munitions factories. Before the war there were just three national factories producing ammunition; by 1916 there were 150. Such a rapid and successful response by the British government is frankly pretty difficult to imagine these days.

The factory straddled the Anglo-Scottish border and ran for nine miles; a vast facility that had more than one hundred miles of rail track and employed some twenty thousand people. Around 70% were female, with 62% aged eighteen or under, and 80% working class. This goes some way to explaining why they were happy to do such dangerous work – the sort that could make their gums rot and their skin yellow. They wouldn't have had many other opportunities.

It was Arthur Conan Doyle who coined the term 'devil's porridge' on his visit to the factory as a war correspondent. This is what he called the cordite, a propellant invented in England and which appeared like spaghetti. "A yard long and a quarter of an inch thick," says my guide. "The girls mixed it by hand in vats like this," he added, leading me to a large metal drum. "They were issued with gloves but hardly any of them wore them."

I am gobsmacked by the pictures of the women that line the walls, wrist-deep in sticky-looking explosives, their eyes and mouths exposed to the fumes. "They weren't allowed to wear a ring," my guide continues. "The metal might have caused a spark and blown up the whole thing." More dangerous work would be hard to come by.

The museum goes on to detail how life was for the workers at the time. This was a new era of freedom for the young women who found work here, and they certainly enjoyed their new higher wages and release from domestic service. The local reverend, W. S. Peebles, complained about the size of the small weekly collection at church compared with what was spent in the local pubs: "£30 to the Lord and £1,000 to the Devil."

In the end, despite Lloyd George upping the tax on booze

significantly, the only answer was for the government to take on all the pubs around the factory. They closed down the roughest pubs in Annan and Carlisle and replaced them with model pubs serving food and offering more wholesome games like billiards and bowls. Licensing hours were set and age restrictions brought in. The great British pub had been turned into what we would recognise today. And there was cheap state beer to boot.

The government also needed to house all these incomers, and so garden cities were built, complete with electric lighting and wide, tree-lined avenues. One of these was Gretna, and on my quick spin through the town it reminds me of Welwyn Garden City close to my home back in England, another planned community designed to be pleasant and, it would seem, unexciting. Gretna is no different: I find an empty children's playground on the green in its centre, and one tiny shop looking forlorn opposite.

Far more famous, of course, is Gretna Green, the ancient village that has long been the first place you come to after crossing the border from England. This was where countless couples, fleeing disapproving relatives and stricter marriage laws in England, were married, from the eighteenth century right up until 1940. Many are said to have arrived in the middle of the night, pursued by angry men on horseback seeking to stop them getting married at all costs.

Today elopements tend to be more about dodging the expense of a gigantic wedding, and so I am far more taken with what lies just outside the town itself; a new Scottish sight that stands on the border as a symbol of unity with England. This is the Auld Acquaintance Cairn, a collection of stones next to the River Sark, which marks the border here. It was created, apparently, using stones from around the United Kingdom, as a love letter to the union. It was meant to be something that would encourage Scots to decide that they wanted to stay in the union with England and, as ideas go, it is a well-meaning one.

But we all know the perils of user-generated content by now, and encouraging people to bring their own stones has led to a mishmash of slogans toppling slowly down over the stones that fill the red sandstone walls of the cairn. *United for good*, one rather menacingly says. *Give us mobile phone signal, not independence*, demands another. A poem etched into a stone inside the cairn entreats Scotland to stay united for the sake of those who died in wars long past.

As so often when it comes to the independence debate, compelling reasons for Scotland to stay are not to be found here. I returned to the car and drove south across the border, three hundred or so miles ahead of me, to contemplate the question still swilling around in my mind: *Just what is it about Scotland?*

Epilogue

When I first heard that Scotland's national animal – as in, officially, on the coat of arms and everything – was the unicorn, I thought I had stumbled into a joke. As I've said before, in my experience the Scots love a good leg-pull, and it is all too easy to fall for a plausible story delivered deadpan.

But the unicorn really is Scotland's national animal and, after travelling around the country for three months, I am not in the least surprised. Because, why not? Why shouldn't a country have a mythical beast as its national animal? Scotland is, after all, a magical place, a land of myths and legends where the truth is often stranger than fiction and every landscape has a story to tell.

I have been enchanted by my time in Scotland. And perhaps now I can finally answer that burning question: why did I feel compelled to come here, as if something magnetic was pulling me north?

It is the fact that, as I travelled, I felt, time and again, that I had found my tribe. Dreams of moving to Barra swirled around my head and finally solidified in the decision to buy a flat in Glasgow. Attendance of a football match, preceded by about the silliest, most passionate party I have ever been to, turned into picking up a Scotland top and (almost) willing this small army of underdogs supported by so many desperate, delighted fans to actually beat

England when the two teams next met. Though maybe just the once.

Scotland has shown herself to be fascinating. From her energetic, wild communities forging a life surrounded by mountains that block out the phone signal and most visitors, right through to her ridiculously beautiful island landscape where everything hinges on the ferry timetable and on getting things done in the lull between the weathers. Writers, musicians, poets, comedians, artists – hundreds have tried to tell the world about this special country to the north of England and yet, down south in London, I get asked more often about where to go in the Maldives, or Tanzania, than where to go in Scotland.

Scotland is worthy of far more than just our holidays, though. It is worthy of our interest and of our respect. This is the country that has not only given the world the television, the telephone and some of its best-loved computer games, but also Harry Potter and Sherlock Holmes, aspirin and wellington boots, the bicycle, radar, the pneumatic tyre and the steam engine. Today Scotland is giving the UK its best source of renewable energy, ideas like the plastic bag charge and minimum alcohol pricing, and by far the best whisky produced anywhere in the world.

In three months I have only scratched the surface. Of course I have only scratched the surface. There are stories in Scotland still waiting to be told, to be heard in local pubs and laughed at in disbelief in welcoming homes. And above all there are people – wonderful, warm, welcoming people who made my trip joyful at every turn.

And if you're English and still wondering about one thing – the one thing we worry about down south, perhaps because we have long held pejorative nicknames for the Scots – then let me tell you now: not one person made even the smallest negative comment about my being English. I didn't encounter one single slight, one ill-judged joke about my ethnicity. If we can't learn anything else from Scotland perhaps we can learn this: tolerance is everything.

As the UK moves into a post-Brexit world I'm not sure there's a more valuable export we could receive from Scotland. Thank you, Scotland, for everything.

Acknowledgements

I would like to thank the Book Guild for believing in my manuscript and for all their hard work in making it presentable and getting it out into the world. Particular thanks to Faye Booth for her meticulous edit.

I would also like to thank Alice Bradbury, who read a very early draft and supplied encouragement, sage advice and enthusiasm for it at every stage.

In researching this book, I spent many months travelling around Scotland and at every turn found warm-hearted, open-minded people who contributed in meaningful ways. Many of them are referenced in the text, but I would also like to thank the Scottish people in general – for being wonderful hosts, hilarious companions and excellent guides. I have travelled to some 50 countries around the world and have of course found wonderful people in every one, but Scotland seems to me to be packed with more than its fair share of them. A hearty *slàinte mhath* to you all.

This book is dedicated to my mum, Susan Jane Ochyra. Mum contracted vasculitis and died on 25th October 2016 at the age of just 62. For a long time before that I had talked about writing a book about Scotland but it was this sudden, life-altering shock that galvanised me into actually doing something about it. I will be eternally thankful that I had talked to her about my ideas before she died. Thank you, mum, for believing in me from the very beginning. Without you, none of this would have been possible and in spirit I know that you were with me every step of the way.

And finally, to my husband, Douglas. Without your endless love and support, it is not overstating it to say that I could not have pulled myself out of the depths of my grief and looked ahead to a brighter future. Since we first met, in a dodgy student bar in Canterbury some twenty years ago, you have believed in me and in my work with a passion that knows no bounds – and have never once complained about me disappearing off to some distant corner of the globe in search of my next travel article either. Without you, I would be lost, in every sense. You are my lighthouse. Thank you, thank you, thank you.

DISCLAIMER

The vast majority of my travels for this book took place in late 2017 and details relating to attractions, hotels, restaurants, etc relate to that time.

Despite often travelling with the much-appreciated assistance of bodies such as the tourist office, hotel chains and tour operators in my usual work as a travel journalist, all travels undertaken for this book were undertaken independently and at my own expense.

REFERENCES AND NOTES

1   Moffat, Alistair, *The Borders: A History of the Borders from Earliest Times*, Birlinn, 2011

2   Oliver, Neil, *A History of Scotland*, Weidenfeld & Nicolson, 2009

3   Winn, Christopher, *I Never Knew That About Scotland*, Ebury Press, 2007

4   The first of any English monarch since Charles II in 1650

5   £126,000 in 1826, calculated into its 2018 value using the Bank of England inflation calculator (http://www.bankofengland.co.uk)

6   http://www.theforthbridges.org

7   Winn, Christopher, *I Never Knew That About Scotland*, Ebury Press, 2007

8   Winn, Christopher, *I Never Knew That About Scotland*, Ebury Press 2007

9   Winn, Christopher, *I Never Knew That About Scotland*, Ebury Press 2007

10   Devine, T., 'The Break-Up of Britain? Scotland and the End of Empire: The Prothero Lecture of the Royal Historical Society' in *Transactions of the Royal Historical Society*, 2006, vol. 16, pp. 163–180, DOI: 10.1017/S0080440106000417

11   Oliver, Neil, *A History of Scotland*, Weidenfeld & Nicolson, 2009

12   According to the *Forbes* World's Billionaires list 2017 (http://www.forbes.com)

13   The Andrew Carnegie Birthplace Museum

14   Global Top 100 companies by market capitalisation, PricewaterhouseCoopers, 31st March 2017 update (http://www.pwc.com/top100)

15 The Andrew Carnegie Birthplace Museum

16 Oliver, Neil, *A History of Scotland*, Weidenfeld & Nicolson, 2009

17 http://www.bbc.co.uk/news/events/scotland-decides/results

18 Happer, Richard, *365 Reasons to be Proud to be Scottish: Magical Moments in Scotland's History*, Portico, 2013

19 *Victoria & Albert: Art & Love*, Royal Collection, Royal Collection Trust, 2012

20 http://www.visitscotland.com/see-do/attractions/castles/scotland-castle-trail/

21 http://features.thesundaytimes.co.uk/richlist/scottish/

22 http://www.scotsman.com/news/politics/aberdeen-overtakes-edinburgh-as-richest-city-1-3826756

23 http://www.aberdeen-harbour.co.uk/about-us/history/

24 Aberdeen Maritime Museum figures from 2008: average full-time wage: Scotland £28,296; Aberdeen £35,959 (source: Bank of Scotland)

25 Figures from the Food and Drink Federation (http://www.fdf.org.uk/exports/ukexports.aspx); total UK food and drink exports for 2016 were £20.2 billion, whisky exports £4.09 billion

26 *Oil & Gas Journal*, http://www.ogj.com

27 Pratt, Joseph A., Priest, Tyler and Castaneda, Christopher J., *Offshore Pioneers: Brown & Root and the History of Offshore Oil and Gas*, Elsevier, 1993

28 NC500 Economic Baseline Study, http://www.hie.co.uk/regional-information/economic-reports-and-research/archive/nc500-economic-baseline-study.html

29 Bryson, Bill, *The Road to Little Dribbling: More Notes from a Small Island*, Black Swan, 2016

30 http://www.ons.gov.uk/peoplepopulationandcommunity/wellbeing/bulletins/measuringnationalwellbeing/localauthorityupdate2015to2016#how-do-people-rate-their-personal-well-being-in-your-area

31 http://www.scotsman.com/lifestyle/outer-hebrides-could-be-linked-together-by-bridge-plan-1-4701642

32 Martin, Martin, *A Description of the Western Isles of Scotland Circa 1695*, Birlinn, 1999

33 http://hebrides.qinetiq.com

34 http://www.hebrides-news.com/south-ford-causeway-21415.html

35 http://ben-nevis.com/information/history/first-ascent/first-recorded-ascent.php